The
Taverners

The Taverners

MARIANO MORILLO B. Ph.D

ARPress
ILLUMINATING IDEAS
EMPOWERING VOICES

ARPress
45 Dan Road Suite 5
Canton, MA 02021

Hotline: 1(888) 821-0229
Fax: 1(508) 545-7580

Ordering Information:
Quantity sales. Special discounts are available on quantity purchases by corporations,associations, and others. For details, contact the publisher at the address above.

Printed in the United States of America.

ISBN-13:   Softcover   979-8-89356-656-7
                   eBook   979-8-89356-657-4

Library of Congress Control Number: 2024903516

TABLE OF CONTENTS

PROLOGUE

Mariano Morillo B. P h.D . Is a writer with ramifications:

Ph.D. in International Law, Master's in Social Work, journalist, poet, storyteller, novelist, and essayist, he once more inspires our knowing and learning interest.

The author's diversity astounds us every day, and now he presents us with his new novel "THE TAVERNERS" for our personal enjoyment of his narrative skills. We may say that this novella is a form of analysis of that generational idiosyncrasy, where violence has sought to triumph over government authorities. For Mariano nothing remains static, and his literature evolves over time, in a way that his readers have already begun to name him as the chronicler of America.

INTRODUCTION

The author in this novel shows us the portraiture of society from the late twentieth and early twenty-first centuries.

In "THE TAVERNERS" we are introduced with a society that succumbs to violence, without those who sustain power being able to prevent it.

Tom, Manolo and You are special agents assigned to fight crime, being forced to confront gang members who do not accept the norms of social ethics, so imbued in the maximum ignorance level of how the good is distinguished, they are inclined to impose the wrong.

To do this, gang members Katiburo and Rey are associated with sectors of the mafia, assuming social predation as their ultimate goal.

However, a spark of hope emanates from that golden moment where Candileja and Tom find a solution through love. Mariano Morillo B., the author of the humanized intellect, definitely, definitely, continues to captivate us with his pen

I

Violence is

a systematic artifact,

that confuses the reason.

Three motorcycles traveling from the north to the south when reaching a curve pair up, almost frictioning, now the drivers frolic between zigzagging pirouettes; All three wear T-shirts under elegant leather vests stamped on the piece that covers the back with a highlighting and colorful vignette that identifies a tiger and at the bottom of the photo there was a sign that read:

Bengal Tigers were young ones that were older than their twenties:

Tom was 29, Rey, 30 and You, the oldest, who looked like the leader of the pack; He was no more than 33. They traveled a little-traversed and unpaved road, implying that they and not others were the owners of the countryside.

A breeze blew on their backs, and the speed-driven dust tended to splatter their bodies.

The sun, that star motivated by global warming, if not for the strong breeze that reduced its heat, surely it would not have hesitated to lash out at the three bodies that dared to challenge it.

The frequent and violent changes of direction of the breeze ran into the treetops, pressing the density of the elusive clouds that had begun to hang low, now converted into shields that forced the retreat of the rays of the sun that bravvely gave way to the storm.

The rain began to bathe the dusty bodies, but the breeze accelerated the water in their backs, making the bodies feel the scourges of nature; there was no escape for shelter.

The military boots they were wearing had started to get soaked, the olive-green backpacks that hung from their backs now weighed twice; They had traveled a long distance before the storm ceased, the density begun to increase,

Finally, they were arriving at a concurrated place, in the distance scattered lights shinning like fireflies announced that the world still existed, it was dark but neither moon nor star could be seen.

They entered the city, turned into a narrow street, a lantern hovered and enveloped the house where they were going, and suddenly they were in front of a beautiful residence, where they entered through a huge entrance gate that remained open.

They stopped, parked the motorcycles, you followed by Tom and Rey, they went to the access door to the interior, stopping and admiring themselves at the carved image of an imperial eagle that decorated the polished mahogany door; It seemed carved by the finest craftsmen in the region.

They rang the bell three times, repeatedly as if urged on by haste.

From inside the house, somebody as young as they go to answer the bell, but stops when opening, suddenly asks:

---- Who? --- Manolo asked from the inside. ----- Your friends from oblivion. --- You said.

He seems to have recognized the voice; however, he opened with a caution; the newcomers had moved out of his range of vision; he looked around silently and found that the three visitors were looking at them with mute smiles; Manolo, who could not hide his embarrassment between happy and surprised, opened his arms seeking to entertain his friends and expressed:

--- Bravo! You, Tom, you all don't fail, I knew you would not keep me waiting! … And he, where did you get him from? ---He said referring to Rey.

--- Ah, he is Rey, he is one of the most seasoned gang members of Los Angeles, he knows so many other gang members and he made himself available to us to relate to them depending on the business. ---- You said.

--- Business? --- Manolo questioned.

--- Yes, yes, the business. Tom said trying to keep Manolo out from going into many details. Ah, yes, the business, come in, you're soaked, get on… wait, I'll find you pajamas while your clothes are drying. --- Manolo said happily.

The three smiling men, reciprocating the invitation entered the living room while Manolo, followed by You, entered a room.

--- What are you doing with that guy, what business are you talking about, does he know who we are? --- Manolo said once more.

---- He neither knows nor should know it, his track was given to us in Washington; one of the contacts from Los Angeles introduced us to him, we must act very well because he thinks we are gang members, so you behaved as such to avoid suspicion. --- You said.

---- But why did they bring him here?

---- It's a long story and we couldn't get rid of him.
--- You explained.

---- Well, let's see, how long can the theater be maintained. --- Manolo said, returning with You.

 With three towels in his hands and a basket containing some clothes that he would later give to his friends.

Manolo handed out the towels to the newcomers and they are taking them and went to the bathroom to remove their wet clothes; not without first continuing to admire the interior clarity of the decoration; Already in the wide bathroom they got rid of the backpacks that they still carried on their backs while Manolos supplied them with still plastic-coated underwear and a pajama for each one, that were inside the basket.

The newcomers got rid of the clothing, emptied the backpacks, unfolding the contents on drying rope for this purpose and put them to dry.

Once the reception ceremony was over, the comments began:

--- Woow man, these last few months have really been progress for you! — Rey dared to comment.

Manolo with a certain humor and showing camaraderie, raised his index finger to his lips, inducing him to silence:

---- Zzzzz, silent so that nobody will hear, is the inheritance of my father, I told them that came to seek my part and I got it without any opposition. All gaping were still standing: --- But ... But ... All this? ... -Tom babbled indicating with the index.

--- Yes, all this and something else ... The truth is that it would be good if you have a seat before you get dizzy. --- Manolo said.

All, as guided by the magic of a melody, sit at the same time but abruptly.

--- Wow, man, I'm still in awe; It seems that they gave you a strong menudo. --- You said.

--- Menudo are coins, and they gave me ... a few bills.

---- And ... Did you spend them all? ... Rey exclaimed with excessive curiosity.

---- No, how could I? I still have as enough as we get fun at the best place here, the Dragon Tavern.

 —Manolo said with some determination.

----Wow, wow, I'm told it's the best place. —Rey said.

While the others speak animatedly, Tom falls silent; so, Manolo motivates him to come out of his lethargy.

--- But what is wrong with you, Tom? you are
so quiet, and now, what bug bit you? ... Manolo
questioned, taking him out of his concentration.

---- No, no, nothing special, I was thinking about
my brother, I shouldn't have stopped going to him
knowing he's here. —Tom said.

--- Oh, is that it? You should not worry, I had
forgotten to tell you that I saw someone who claims
to know him and he told me that he is fine, I wanted
to ask him where he was and he did not know how
to answer me but I instructed him that if he saw him
again to tell him that you would be at this address, I
think that you will be able to find him without much
effort. — Manolo said trying to cheer him up.

Tom stood up with a start:

--- How come he told you that he saw him, and
you don't know where he is living? Tell me where I
can find the guy who told you he knew about him,
in what place? ... Manolo interrupting him tried to
justify his statement:

--- Calm down Tom, I did not ask him where he was
staying, but if he sees him again, he will give him the
message, and he will come this way, I sent him this
address.

--- What? did you give him the address? You shouldn't have, if he comes, Tom will go with him. —You said.

--- What does it matter if he takes this brat? --- Rey said.

The violence took control of Tom, who unleashes a fist on him, causing him to roll on the ground.

--- Rogue, I told you not to call me a brat. Tom expressed, somewhat upset.

Rey standing up tried to return his fist, but You's intervention stalled his intention.

---- Enough, stupids, save your violence for those who attack us, let's not harm each other, you, Tom, don't let what you did happen again, I don't like that divisive action, what you just did not only do you confirm as a brat, but as arrogant; we will not allow this to happen again. --- Shouted You.

---- Forget that and let's have fun, you will need your strength. —Manolo said.

--- Yeah, that's what we have to do. --- Rey corroborated, without apparent rancor.

--- Then, I will show you, my motorcycle. - Manolo said while there would be a door where they glimpsed a luxurious racing motorcycle, with a nickel-plated strip combined with black and red colors, which when seen by the newcomers, kept the great astonishment in all except Tom, who still had his nerves going.

----- Weet woooo, what a beauty! —You said...

---- Oops, it seems that your treasure was not little. – Rey expressed, with the curiosity of a thief.

---- Forget it, let's go have fun. And do you like it, Tom? – Asked Manolo.

--- Oh, yes, of course ... it's very pretty. — Claimed Tom.

--- Well now let's go out, let's go to the Dragon Tavern —Manolo   said while he proceeded to take his motorcycle where his friends were, who at the same time limited themselves to heating theirs motors while Manolo close the door of his residence; When they were able to turn on their motors to go out, each one mounted the one that corresponded to him and went out to the street, from where they proceeded to make the route that would lead them to the place where they had planned to go, a few minutes later, they were in the much-acclaimed den.

II

Life is a riddle that

we must decipher without fear.

They had reached the Dragon Tavern; they were parked in the available allocated space; It gave the impression that there was no other type of transportation other than motorcycles; all the space was occupied by them.

They proceeded to enter the interior of the den and found the space of the light reflection of different lights that changed per second concomitantly.

Some of those regular visitors used to amuse themselves by resorting to the different modes of the ambience and at that moment many of them enjoyed dancing and the others gulping down liquors, some standing in front of the counter, and others sitting at the different round tables.

The abruptly and arbitrary entry of the newcomers aroused the interest of those present, and a gang that was chatting there felt challenged.

Those gang members had the great reputation of being the most feared in the environment, and they coincided that night when they made that place their ephemeral abode.

They wore short hair, their Vestments were decorated by the head of a huge black cat, with that they paid homage to their name, they were called cats.

While somebody socialized, as much as the environment allowed, standing or sitting, the others had fun dancing "rock and roll".

At the table of the curious, there were five women and five men who made up that group, who that night frequented the Dragon Tavern.

Women remained seated facing their companions, and they were the first to closely follow the presence of the newcomers, and some of the women, above the vigilance of their companions, could not control their flirting impulses.

In that way, the newcomers, before the waiter indicated where they should sit, chose a side from where they could control the action of any movement.

You tried to put his feet up on the table, however, seeing himself admonished by Manolo who whispered in his ears how convenient it would be not to be unprepared, he adjusted his body in a different way.

Rey clapped twice, and inmediately the waiter appeared.

--- Tell me young man, how can I be useful to you. — asked the newly convoked one.

--- Thank you, gentle waiter, who knows. --- You said, with no other intention than to sell the image of a low gang member.

--- Bring beer for everyone. --- Manolo said.

--- Very well. --- The waiter nodded as he went to bring the order.

At that moment Katiburo, who was called the one who led the cats, made a marked signal to the waiter, who quickly moved to where he was, who, noticing his proximity to him, had subjected the waiter to an impertinent question:

--- Who are those whippersnappers? --- Katiburo asked, with a hint of impertinence.

Before answering, the waiter looked at the Bengal Tigers with disguised caution, and proceeded to say:

---- I really don't know, they are new here, it's the first time I've seen them around here. --- The waiter replied, heading back to the counter.

--- Indeed, maybe they are not from around here. --- Katiburo alluded.

--- No, you already confirmed it. --- Kent said, the second of the Cats.

The best option would be to inquire; You girls, you have work, we need to know who they are, find a way to attract them; so, go to flirt, I have spoken! --- Katiburo affirmed, giving a spanking to Kenya, who like a zeppelin had already stood up, before the others.

The girls had not finished listening to the mandate and ipso facto he was seen prowling their table; Kenia, a personal friend of Katiburo; she was the first to introduce herself, in such a simple way that she gave the impression of being the expert in public relations; So, let's see her start her conversation with Tom:

--- Hello, gentleman, what's up! (1) would you like to dance? —She asked.

--- I'm really very flattered but not, thank you, I don't want to dance; I'm not in the mood for that. --- He said.

--- Gee, Gee Tom, how dare you despise this trilogy of carnations? --- Manolo said joking.

---- Thank you dear; may we sit? --- Kenia asked.

Greeting which means how are you?

---- Of course, yes! --- You affirmed.

At Manolo's indication, the waiter approached, adding other chairs around the circular tables. The dolls sat down; and they were distributed as follows; Kenia next to You, Mily next to Rey and Yuly next to Manolo. The waiter approaches, now he brings in his hands a tray with seven beers previously ordered, and a few glasses, in case any of them wanted to be decent, but in fact he did not expect it.

---- Here is the order, and their respective glasses. --- Said.

--- Let me drink directly from the bottle. --- You ordered without further ado.

--- We are seven ones ---- Manolo said.

---- Count six; I don't want beer. --- Tom affirmed.

--- Well done--- You said jokingly --- Alcohol is for adults.

Tom does not pay attention; On the other hand, You acted without moderation and in a single sip You drinks half a beer, which activates your discernment to act and respond to your guests; When each of them had already ingested two beers, a feeling of disinhibition had seized them and then You, taking the initiative, threw his arm around Kenya and stroked her, their nerves had twitched when suddenly the lack of adrenaline control leading to the kiss, Manolo and Rey who saw what happened, realizing that there would be no resistance, they imitated it, being reciprocated by both Mily and Yuly.

However, the cats, those neighboring felines, felt frustrated in the mission assigned to the females that accompanied them; anger and jealousy were stronger than their discretion and standing up they went to the table of their new adversaries; who approaches without being noticed by those, but Tom, only Tom notices that malicious presence just in time, however, he cannot avoid Kent's angry out of control, who without warning, spilled the contents of the table on the floor, and where glasses and bottles splashed on passionate lovers, but before sweeping the tables with the hands and without a broom, let's see with what intention of the heart he expressed himself:

--- Damn group of rats; you will see who we are the "Cats"
--- Kent mumbled through clenched teeth; However, You, that master tiger of street violence nimbly moved away from Kenya and like a jungle feline hungry to devour its prey, he launched himself on his opponent, knocking him down with a punch, which motivated the intervention of the other gang members and there they were. rolling on the floor.

In a corner Kent, now was trying to strangle Tom:

--- Let me go, damnit--- Tom said, looking for a way to free himself from Kent's grasping tentacles; and he achieves it by placing the military boots in the center of the belly, bringing it to a forced landing on the floor.

The victory that the cats believed assured now eluded them; the Bengal Tigers reacted against his opponents, Katiburo who had put his hand in his mouth felt disappointed, he had just felt his sharp teeth, you had bitten him making him meow like a real feline.

Kraw strucks a punch at Manolo's jaw that made him taste the floor, but when trying to get on top, Manolo stretched his leg from the ground and placed his right foot on his chest, pushing him strongly backwards, going to lean on a table where there was a group consuming and whose members did not hesitate on pushing it to the center of battle; while Rey sounding his open hands over Kurt's ears -the ungrateful cat- had left him exhausted on the floor, many of the presents were impressed, others a bit scared; they were like warriors on the battlefield; the fight had intensified.

The Bengala Tigers and the Stray Cats were fighting a duel; From the fists they passed to the objects, chairs and bottles crossed the air, screams of terror and suddenly… screams of women and in the surroundings police sirens; the men of "order" were not far away.

The escape door was narrowing, everyone was trying to get out from behind, now some were on the ground and were being stomped on; lthe artificial railings of the bar that had been lowered blocked access to the bottles; the blood was not like a river, but some were already injured.

When the cats rolled on the ground, the Bengala Tigers knew was wise to get away from there; without policemen being able to prevent it, as striped panthers they jumped on the motorcycles, the cats got up and tried to follow him, however inside the Dragon Tavern, before they could go out to the parking lot, Katiburo prevented it:

--- Forget it, it seems that the police are prowling closely, and you might notice, we will meet them soon.

Rosy, Mily and Yuly -still confused- had limited themselves to contemplating what was happening, they approached to clean their friend's face, who -even full of bruises- did not stop suppressing them.

Bengala tigers had drifted away from the Dragon Tavern; and they took different routes, Manolo and Rey had deviated on one side, while You and Tom had gone on the other.

III

Logical reasoning induces

to fair discernment.

The next day they had woken up with the fatigue of the previous night: it was a Saturday, October 22, when the sunlight was reflected inside the house, the three rooms had been distributed evenly, however Tom preferred to sleep on the sofa in the living room.

They had used up a part of their rest time, then in the afternoon they were arriving around a supermarket, thinking that while You and Manolo went looking for some food, Rey and Tom would remain in the access street.

Then Tom, staying watching the motorcycles of the others, while Rey made a circular turn on his motorcycle; Resulting that at that precise moment someone with whom they had never shared, tried to cross the street, having chosen to block her path, circled around her, and then when he thought she was dizzy, he was stopped in front of her; Then realizing he discovered that she bear a strong resemblance to Mily, one of the women of the previous night, with whom he had entertained himself; he tried to stop her:

--- Wow, what beauty; You look better today than last night, why don't we smooch? —Said, with an unusual morbidity.

---- I think you are mistaking me for someone, I've never seen you before in my life. --- Candileja said, which was the name by which she was recognized.

---- You look like a faded flower, but I wouldn't mind you taking a ride.

--- I am not used to talking to a stranger and it is better that you leave me alone. --- Candileja said.

--- I neither want nor to intend to leave you alone. --- Rey said with the intention of annoying her.

--- Let me pass. --- Candileja begged him.

Tom who has been aware of what was happening, abruptly intervened: ---- You already heard her; she wants you to give way to her and leave her alone. --- Tom said.

Rey, who, silently angry with Tom, was waiting for a reason to justify himself, he believed the moment to act was opportune, and like a thoughtless cat, he jumped violently and in surprise from the motorcycle, ready to admonish Tom:

---- Plague; Who asked for your opinion? —Rey replied.

--- How can you see anyone did it; but she has asked you to give way, right miss? …

--- Candileja, I'm known as Candileja. --- She stated that she was still ecstatic and surprised.

--- What if I refuse? --- Rey claimed, who defiantly blocked the path to Candileja again.

--- Then I will be forced to intervene with force. --- Tom claimed.

--- You, and how many more, coward? - Said Rey, jumping abruptly on Tom and giving him a strong punch to the jaw that led him to touch the ground.

Tom, who coming to his senses, a bit surprised by the unexpected punch, placed a kick in the chest of his opponent that led him to kiss the asphalt.

Candileja that still had not moved from where she was, more surprised, covered her open mouth with the palm of her hand, she was stunned, she did not believe that her presence generated that altercation.

Rey had become dangerous, now he exhibited a knife that was rotated from one hand to another, returning on Tom, with much more violence, who still trying to avoid him to avoid the punch, could not block the tackle, receiving a wound in an arm.

Rey, when realized what caused to Tom, when he saw him bleed, was shocked and terrified, he jumped on his motorcycle and fled.

--- Oh, I'm sorry; the fault is mine; Why have you done this for me? --- she said while she is being even more confused.

---- It's nothing; it's just a dirty trick. --- Tom said, while bleeding considerably.

--- You are bleeding too much; I will take you home. ---Said, while he removed from her neck a handkerchief that she used as a scarf, and which she proceeded to use as a tourniquet that blocked the flow of blood.

--- Okay, thanks, I'll get over it. --- Tom said.

---- But we have to stop the bleeding. --- Candileja insisted.

Tom, reflecting on the insistence, agreed:

---- Okay, thank you, I appreciate it. --- Said.

--- And do you plan to leave the motorcycle? --- Candileja Asked.

--- I'll be back for it; secure the motorcycle to the post, put its padlock, then I'll get it back. --- He said giving to her the padlock key.

Tom began to weaken; Candileja led him to her car that was a few meters away in the supermarket parking lot.

--- We have to get there before it's too late; he has lost too much blood. ---she said while driving at high speed.

Tom, without strength, tries to keep himself balanced; When they are arriving at her domicile, Candileja parked the car in the marquee, from where she drove him inside the house, meeting with her mother, Mrs Martha, who at that moment was leaving her room:

--- What happened Candileja, who is he? --- Mrs. Martha asked.

---- There is no time to explain it to you; bring me a bandage please.

Mrs. Martha obeyed her daughter's command, and immediately handed her the bandage.

She helped him settle into the furniture, and at one point he managed to stop the bleeding by applying a compress, and then she proceeded to clean and heal the wound, then discovering that the wound itself was not that serious, it was a simple scratch, but on the way, the loss of blood had weakened him.

Then, with the assistance of Mrs. Martha, her mother, she gets stabilized. When she deemed him safe, she made a phone call to a friend's clinic:

---- Good afternoon, hello doctor, it's me Candileja, is Robert here? ... No? then I need you to come at my house urgently; no, it's not that, I'll explain here; well yes, there is somebody here, wounded in a vein, yes, I got to stop the bleeding; okay thanks, I'll be waiting.

Hanging up the phone, she discovered that Tom had collapsed on the piece of furniture.:

--- Oh, now he's passed out; Mommy come and help me take him to the room.

With Mrs. Martha's help, they transferred him to the adjoining room that had already been set up for this purpose.

She put her hand into the bowl, took the key to the motorcycle, and handed it to Rudy, her only brother at the young age of 17, he was still young, and told him:

--- Rudy, take this key, bring a blue motorcycle that is parked on Calle Pino del Olmo, in the parking lot of the Super Mercado Opera del Hogar; Come straight here and bring it with me. --- Candileja said.

--- Who is he, what happened to him? --- The boy questioned curiously as he caught the key between his fingers.

--- I'll explain later, let's go now. --- Ordered Candileja.

---- Okay. --- Rudy argued, walking away at once.

The young boy leaving and Doctor Olmedo arriving:

--- What has happened Candileja, where is the wounded man?--- Asked Dr. Olmedo.

--- Hello, Dr. Olmedo, good that you have arrived, come here, the wounded man has lost a lot of blood and has collapsed, he exposed his life to defend me, from somebody who wanted to assault me, I feel responsible. ---- Candileja said to the doctor who without further ado followed her to the room where Tom was.

When Dr. Olmedo looked at him, he took his pulse and saw that he was still alive, so without investigating deeply, he changed the bandage that Candileja put on him, took a deep breath and asked:

--- Tell me, is he your relative? --- Dr. Olmedo questioned intentionally.

Not exactly doctor, but as I mentioned, that wound he received due to me, he tried to defend me from someone who was bothering me. --- Candileja reaffirmed.

-- Ah, I see; he'll have to rest for a couple of days until he recovers. --- Stated Dr. Olmedo.

---- Alright I'll take care of him. --- Candileja assured him.

--- Well then, it's good to let him conscious. --- Dr. Olmedo asserted; he tried to wake him from fainting; he moistened a tow in a medicine giving it to the wounded man to sniff, who at the time of inhaling was conscious again.

--- Hey, hey, hey, hey! Where am I, who are you? --- Tom said.

--- Don't worry, you're extremely well catered; I am your doctor, and here, Miss Candilejas is your host and protector.--- Doctor Olmedo affirmed.

---- Aaaaaaah … yes, I remember, thank you very much Miss Candilejas, now I must go. --- Tom said trying to move from the bed where he was lying.

---- No, no, no. You must rest for at least three days. --- Dr. Olmedo warned him.

----- But… -- Tom tried to replicate.

---- No, no buts, don't worry, stay in bed now you are my guest, if it had not been for me, none of this would have happened. --- Candileja said.

--- You don't have to blame yourself for anything, if something's going to happen, it happens. --- Tom said.

--- What goes around comes; So now everything is my responsibility, you can rest without worry; I already sent my brother for the motorcycle, he knows how to drive well, so calm down. --- Candileja reaffirmed him.

---- Thank you very much! ---- Tom decided to say that, as a token of his great appreciation.

Dr. Olmedo injected Tom with an anti-tetanus penicillin and then wrote some prescriptions that he gave to Candileja:

--- Here are these two recipes, this one is for anti-inflammatories and this one is for treating of pain.--- He said while extending them to Candileja.

---- Very good dr. Olmedo, I'll take care of it, Thank you .--- Candileja affirmed.

---- Well, now I have to go; I'll be back in two or three days, see you soon. --- Dr. Olmedo said as he left.

--- Bye for now, doctor, thank you.--- Tom said.

--- Goodbye Tom, follow my instructions.

--- I'll walk you out. --- Candileja said behind him.

 After closing the door, she returned to the room where Tom was, and introduced her mother with his guest.

They mobilized him to take off his vest and then went out to prepare something to eat.

Just at the moment when Rudy unchained Tom's motorcycle, You and Manolo came out with some bags in their hands but when they saw that the unknown young man tried to remove Tom's motorcycle, they chose to question him:

--- Wait, boy, what do you intend to do with that motorcycle? --- Manolo asked.

--- His owner asked me to take it away. --- Rudy answered without remorse.

---- Explain us better; what's happening? --- You interfered.

---- Who are you, do you know him? —Rudy asked.

---- Yes, that's why we ask you, he is our friend. --- Manolo said.

---- Oh, if so, nice to meet you; I'm Rudy. --- Rudy said introducing himself.

---- Nice to meet you, I am You and he is Manolo; now that we meet, tell me what you intend to do with that motorcycle. --- You said, looking for an explanation.

--- I already told you, his owner asked me to take him where he is, something happened, and he is at my house. --- Rudy said.

--- What happened? where is your house and what is he looking for there? — Manolo asked persistently.

--- Well ... he would have to explain it to you, if you want, I will take you where he is, follow me. ---- Rudy exclaimed.

 ---- Wait a minute boy. —You said, while they arranged the bags that they carried in their hands in double bags that were secured on the motorcycles.

--- Already--- Manolo said.

The three men had turned on their motorcycles almost at the same time; they followed the young man and did not stop until they arrived.

--- Wait now, let me notify your presence. --- Rudy said while he entered to his house, leaving his companions in front of the door.

Inmediately, He appeared again accompanied by Martha and Candileja.

--- How do we help you? --- Candileja said.

--- We saw that the young man here was trying to remove our friend's motorcycle and we were interested to know what happened to him, and where is him? --- Replied You.

Candileja explained all the details of what happened, let him know that he was sleeping because he was under the effects of some painkillers; they insisted on seeing him and asked Candileja that when Tom woke up -and was in a condition to listen- to tell him that they were seeing him there, and that they would see him again; then they go back the same way they come, towards the house they lived with Manolo.

IV

From the noble soul, solidarity springs up

on every existential plane.

The next day the humidity dominated the environment; It had dawned cloudy, and the day was a bit hot; when Candileja entered the room where Tom was recovering, she couldn't help an air of satisfaction under her skin, she was really trying to hide her feelings; A growing tingle came over her, for a moment she silently stared at the wounded man who was still under sedation and sleeping like a child.

Candileja took the opportunity and placed a vase with a bouquet of fresh roses on the table next to the head of the wounded man and then left the room again; in the living room, for a moment, she was immobile and thought about the fate blows, in the way in how episodes of human existence are unexpectedly generated and developed every day.

Then she thought about what would be the purpose of destiny, when bringing into her life and in that circumstance, that stranger man, however a breath of hope gave calm to her soul, he had freed her from that unexpected moment of terror and even.

He fought for her, he could have been able to take advantage of her, but he didn't, and that gave her confidence.

Then she also thought about how she would justify herself in front of her father if he arrived and found that stranger young occupying one of the rooms of the house; in that she again experienced the magical breath that instantly wrapped her, and she thought about herself and Tom and pronounced as if she were talking to another self:

--- Could it be that I am falling in love? How can it be? Oh, my heart, don't do this to me! --- She said patting the left side of his chest.

Then she continued absorbed in her monologue; determined to find out what she really felt for Tom:He does not look bad, he's brave, Young and I like him, but I know my father, I know that he is going to reproach me; He is so ambitious that he only thinks about money, he is not satisfied with what he has and wants me to marry Adolfo, however I will neither allow him to force my feelings, nor ruin my happiness. What does he know about my heart?

Besides, I don't like Adolfo; instead Tom … even though I don't know him, he catches my attention, I think I'm in love with him.--- Candileja monologized in a kind of self-venting, until Rudy's unexpected entrance brought her back from her overwhelming discernment.

--- Take it, sister, here is the key; Wow… what an amazing motorcycle! It is fantastic and beautiful. --- Rudy said admiring the pleasure of that experience, while he extended the key to Candileja.

---- It's not mine but I'm glad you liked it. --- Candileja replied.

Thanks: I'll tell him to lend it to me for a ride on Sunday… But and where is him? --- Rudy asked.

--- He's in the guest room. ---Candileja said.

---- Oh, and how did he get that wound? --- Rudy asked.

When Candileja tried to answer him, Mrs. Martha intervened:

--- Rudy, don't ask so many questions!" Mrs. Martha said.

--- Okay, now that mom is here, I'll tell you ... When I was coming back from trying on the dress in Plaza de la Opera, when I went to the car to come back here, someone blocked my path and started to bother me and if Tom don't come out to defend me, I don't know what would have happened; The criminal was armed and caused that wound causing him to hemorrhage, so it was my duty to assume the responsibility of helping him and I could not leave him abandoned, I brought him here.

--- What if daddy comes and finds him? --- Rudy asked.

--- This time he will have to listen to me. --- Exclaimed Candileja.

--- Don't worry daughter, I'll talk to him. —Mrs. Martha said.

--- It's okay mom, whatever you say. --- Exclaimed Candileja.

At that moment, Ana Casilda arrived, Mrs. Martha's eldest daughter, and Candileja's sister., who has been related to Robert, Tom's brother but unaware that he is his brother-in-law; upon entering she kisses her mother and Candileja, and hugs Rudy:

---- Hello, how have you been, and dad, hasn't he arrived? --- Asked.

---- Not yet you…? you arrived early. --- Questioned and affirmed at the same time Mrs. Martha.

 ---- Yes, Mom, remember that I left early because there was a lot of work accumulated, it was necessary to prepare the payment of the miners, because they had three days of late pay; By the way, haven't you called Robert? --- Ana Casilda asked.

--- I don't think so, I called him at the clinic, and he was in surgery, Dr. Olmedo came in his place. ---- Candileja answered.

---- Did he come? … For what? --- Ana asked curiously as she handed her mother some books that she was carrying in her hand and leaned down on the sofa in the living room.

--- Let's go to your room, I'll tell you there. --- Candileja said.

They went to Ana's room where he explained everything that had happened with luxurious details.

Shortly afterwards, Candileja went to the guest room at the precise moment when Tom was beginning to wake up; he sat in a chair facing the bed; discovering that Tom was contemplating her in silence and still half asleep, as if he did not know her:

---- Where am I? … -- He said looking across the room, as if searching for an object he could identify.

 ---- What? Did you forget again? You still don't recognize me? You are still right there when the doctor treated you, you were wounded for defending me and I brought you to my family's house; you fainted and the doctor recommended rest, then he sedated you to rest, and it is now when you wake up again. --- Candileja said.

--- Well, thank you, now I remember — He looks at the bandage over the wound, while arguing — that scoundrel Rey hurt me… --- Then he gazes into her eyes and asks her —

--- What is your name? --- Tom asked.

--- Candileja Armendariz. --- Said.

--- It's a beautiful name --- Said and Added —My name is Tom Alexander.

--- I know it; forgive me, I had to check your identifications, you were wouded and I did not take you to the hospital, I called friends from a clinic and the doctor you saw the first time you woke up treated you in private; I also see that you share the same last name of a doctor that is like member of the family, I mean Dr. Robert Alexander.--- Candileja said.

--- Did you say Robert Alexander?... --- Tom asked.

--- That's right, I mean him, do you know him? --- Candileja asked curiously.

---- Yes, I think it's him -Tom said, in thoughtful action as if he's connecting the dots.

---- He is my brother-in-law. --- Candileja Exclaimed.

--- Your brother-in-law ... You mean your boyfriend's brother? --- Tom asked, trying to get to a point.

---- I don't have a boyfriend; I mean my sister's brother. --- Candileja replied.

--- Does your sister respond to the name of Ana Casilda? --- Tom asked serenely.

---- How do you know? --- Candileja insisted.

---- Robert is my brother --- Tom exclaimed.

---- How is it possible? ... Destiny, circumstances or coincidence, that's life.

Do you know my sister? ---- Candileja asked.

 ---- No, but Robert has told us a lot about her, he said he would take time to introduce her into the family. --- Tom replied.

Candileja, a little confused, moves her head from side to side as if denying the circumstance; Tom tries to support himself on the hand of the injured arm, but the pain does not allow it:

----Ouch! --- The moan emitted by Tom expresses his feeling, before the condition of the pain:

---- Don't lean, you can bleed, I'll help you get up. —Ipso facto, Candileja offered him her shoulder while Tom was trying to balance himself, for a moment Tom faltered as if he were going to fall, in her eagerness to hold him in balance causes a scene where the two face each other, they stare at each other as if they were going to kiss but Candileja looks away as if confused and seeking to evade what happened, slowly withdraws from him while arguing:

--- One moment, I am going to introduce you to Ana, your sister-in-law. --- Candileja said as she left the room.

Shortly after, Tom was introduced to Ana Casilda, at the same time that he began to experience the comfort of a family encounter.

Ana is the oldest of the three siblings; She is an administration executive of "Gold West" a multinational company that exploits the country's gold deposits, for five years she has been in charge of operations, she is the main executive based in the capital and she is the one who issued the payment orders to Nacional level of employment that operated in the country, but despite her duties, she had never wanted to get away from her family.

She had met Robert Alexander, a reputable surgeon at an social security seminar for employment, because the clinic under his direction supplied the security of the Gold West employment management nationwide.

Ana had insisted that Candileja went to university as she had done, in the career of business administration.

Martha, her mother was in charge of the house and her father was dedicated to the transportation business; he owned three dump trucks that he leased to other companies to haul sand for construction work.

Medium restored now; Tom talked with his sister-in-law Ana Casilda with such freedom that he had already been able to return to the living room leaving the room where he had to remain in his state of forced prostration; then the memory arose that he had left his motorcycle tied up at the scene of the incident, he had forgotten that Candileja had entrusted Rudy with the favor to go and rescue it:

--- But have I not asked about my motorcycle again? ... if I lose it, I will surely have to work hard to buy another. --- He said with intention of having someone inform him about it.

Then Candileja who was returning from one of the rooms could hear him, she went ahead to answer him:

--- I told you before, Tom, that I commissioned Rudy to take care of your motorcycle, and he went to look for it, the motorcycle is in the marquee, so don't worry that it is well guarded, besides, for now you will not be able to drive it until your wounds heal; We haven't been able to locate Robert, but a message has already been left for him, so that he will know you are here. —Candileja said.

--- Well thank you very much; I'm really grateful. --- Tom exclaimed.

---- You do not have to worry about anything, you are part of the family and if we had offered to support you even though we did not know your origin; now that we have confirmed it, with much more reason. --- Ana Casilda exclaimed.

--- Thank you very much once again. ---Tom said.

--- Also, Rudy loves the pattern and the color; he has been so motivated that he is determined to get one when he turns twenty. - Candileja said.

--- Well then, I'll have someone to ride with me. --- Tom said.

--- Ana Casilda, I am very happy; of meeting you, Robert had told me a lot about you, and he was curious, but I never imagined that he would be this way. --- Tom said.

That's the way life is, often calculating and unpredictable. --- Ana Casilda answered.

--- And Rudy, where is he? - Tom asked

He is at karate practices. --- Ana Casilda replied.

---- Oh, so even karate fighter and all. --- Tom said.

--- It's a way to keep him focused, it's like an after-school program. --- Candileja added.

--- Ah, that's good, the capital is not like the province and here you have to be prepared, in every way. —Tom exclaimed.

--- That's it. --- Ana Casilda assured.

At that, Mrs. Martha appeared, and when she saw the three of them reunited, she intervened in the conversation:

--- Do you feel better young boy? --- Martha asked.

--- Yes, lady, my pain has calmed. --- Tom said.

--- I am glad that you are better; I would like to thank you for what you did for Candileja. --- Martha expressed.

--- Do not worry, I am one of the people who will never be indifferent to any type of abuse. --- Tom claimed.

---- Mom, don't you know the last thing I just discovered? ---Candileja questioned.

---- You have not told me anything; Let me know what's going on. --- Martha said looking at Tom while smiling.

--- Tom and Robert are brothers. --- Candileja affirmed as if internally enjoying the information she had just supplied.

---- Are you kidding, Candileja? --- Martha said with a hint of disbelief.

--- No, mom, how do you think I'm going to joke with something so serious. ---Candileja said.

---- Yes, mom, they are brothers. --- Ana Casilda confirmed.

--- That's right, Robert is my brother, it's just him and me, he came to this state, and I stayed there studying, and accompanying my father and mother. --- Tom explained.

---- Well, I'm glad to hear that, welcome and this is still your home. --- Martha said.

---- Thank you. --- Tom said, while he exchanged a knowing smile with Candileja.

V

Music being the soul of the people,

listening to it and not blushing

is like being matter without spirit.

Meanwhile, at their residence, Manolo, You and Rey discuss what happened with Tom:

--- Rey, you're really a fucking stupid; Two days have passed, and Tom has not just shown up, we saw him the day you caused the injury, however today we returned, and we forgot the house, we went to another place, the houses there are all similar, we did not ask for the phone number and he doesn't call yet, all because of you. --- You said.

---- Stop, You, I told you that he attacked me, and I defended myself, I accidentally wounded him and ran because with the genius that he brought, if I stopped, maybe I would have been killed.

--- Well, what are we going to do? If he found his brother, probably he'll forget about us; I lied to him

42

and told him that I had seen him so that he would not worry, but I don't even know him. — Manolo said trying to pretend in front of Rey.

You are moving from one side to the other radically faces Rey:

---- I insist that this scoundrel is the culprit. ---- He says while strongly pushing King.

--- You brute, if you push me again, I will take your eyes out. --- Rey warned You.

---- Enough, stop the fight and let's think about what we will do; Cats can appear at any moment and if they find us separated they could make it difficult for us.

Rey remained motionless and -like a flash- he received the inclination to betrayal.

--- Oh, I think they just gave me an ideal idea; Surely if I become friends with them and join their gang they won't fight with me, right? --- Rey thought until he was interrupted by Manolo.

---- What will be the thought that invades your neurons? --- Manolo commented.

----- Aahh, me? ... nothing, nothing, I thought that the next time we measure the cats they will regret forever.

----Very optimistic of you, I hope you are not the regrettable one. ---- You said.

--- Why do you say that? ... I will take my precautions, for now I will go out to warm up my motorcycle and then we will see what happens. --- Rey said.

---- Well, try not to stray too far, so they won't find you alone. --- You said.

--- I will know how to do it. ---- Rey said, While going out.

When Rey left the place, Manolo and You exchanged a look of uncertainty, while You warned:

--- We have to take care of that traitor; he is up to something. -You exclaimed.

--- Do you think he discovered us? - Manolo asked.

--- Possibly not, if he had, we would already know, his tendency to felony would give him away.

Actually, Manolo and You, were not far from the truth, since Rey had decided to implement his plan; without noticing the risk that he could take, he went with the conscience of the felon to the tavern of the Dragon.

After traveling the distance recorded in the marked time, he parked his motorcycle where the others were, went to the fun room and Mily was there, the one that a few weeks before she had shared with him and that with great diligence had come out to meet him.

--- Wowowo, cute; you really provoke my soul. - Rey said with a certain mischief (2) seeing her in front of him.

- And how can I help you? hottie. - Mily replied, unable to feign her flirtation.

- Uh, for everything hot; (3) something like to redesign the map of love on your skin. - Rey said in the spirit of praising the conversation.

- Hottie, (4) look at how you have turned out to be a poet, your words provoke me, if you feel like that, follow me, and let no more be said. —Mily added.

-- Uh, how aggressive you are, stunner, (5) Well, here I go. - Rey said, as he realized that the room was maintained without a large crowd of people, so his opponents had not yet arrived.

(2) Baseness, vileness / Youngster's mischief (3) beautiful (4) very elegant (5) Beautiful, pretty, Beautiful, in Mexico, and Prostitute in the Dominican Republic, the use in this work refers to Mexican regionalism.

He walked in the direction where Mily led him; They went up to the second floor, and stopped in front of a door where she inserted a key, opened the door and entered a beautifully decorated room; It seemed like a semi-studio where she resided; Mily came up to him and said:

- I think I know you, where have I seen you? ... ah, of course, you were here before ... Uh, you really are daring; If they find you, it is certain that they will make you mincemeat. - Warned Mily.

- Don't worry, stunner, (6) I come to negotiate; I have the intention of moving to the other side, and if they don't accept me, they lose it. - Rey said.

(6) Beautiful, phenomenal, wonderful. Wow, you're the type of man that turns me on- Mily said as she put her arms around him.

He kissed him on the lips as she walked away and offered him a drink that Rey gladly accepted; they toasted them and then they hugged again, they kissed passionately again, and then had sex.

Half an hour had passed since the moment they came up; While Mily rested, he got up, placed the sum of fifty dollars on a nightstand, and prepared to leave the room.

When he returned, he found that those whom he wanted to meet were already in the room as usual, the waiter who did not recognize him when he went upstairs, when looked at him squarely, he was exacerbated.

The cats were gathered, in ecstatic in a corner of the room; the music that was playing stopped abruptly when Rey entered the place.

They stood up as if Rey's presence had affected the sound, Kent had recognized him; However, before he could get close, Rey ran like a cannonball, holding him by the neck, Rey put Kent on his back, and with a knife touching his throat as a threat he warned:

---- If someone moves, it is a fact that his friend loses his neck; I want to make peace with you and I am even willing to go over to your side, always you give me some guarantee that later you will not betray me; So I come in peace. I want to talk to the leader. ---- Rey said still threatening Kent.

---- What do you want, how do we know that you come in search of peace and that the pact you offer will be fulfilled? --- Katiburo said.

---- You can see it, if I did not come willing to fulfill the pact, do you think that I would come helplessly to face you, even knowing that I am putting my life at risk? --- Rey replied.

---- You are right; I know you are brave, but to be a member of this gang you have to demonstrate your ability to sacrifice something, that is, you will have to go through a testing process. ---- Katiburo said

---- And… If I go through that process, will you keep your word? --- Rey questioned trying to be sure.

---- Yes, for our honor. ---- Katiburo replied.

---- Swear to me for something else; many times, for us honor is not enough. ---- Rey said, looking for a way to compromise.

 ---- For my life. ---- Katiburo exclaimed.

---- Agreed! --- Rey said, as he released and pushed Kent on them and added --- Okay, now, what do you want me to do? --- he said.

--- You will have to face Kraw on an equal status. --- Katiburo said.

---- I accept. ---- Rey said.

Although Kraw is scary for being the strongest in the gang, that doesn't seem to intimidate Rey, and it should; he was a person of great musculature; tall and potbellied; Besides, he did not wait, he seized a thick chain that he brandished in the air, starting the bloody combat; they looked like two titans raffling a gazelle.

Rey faced him with his cutting weapon, or rather, with that shining Sevillana; which Kraw used as

a reason to try to leave him without a weapon,
He had loosed three chains strikes in the air, one
after the other. Rey stepped backwards and in an
unexpected action crisscrossed him under the legs,
getting to knock him down, seizing in an oversight
of the chain; However, in a defensive action, Kraw
turning had managed to throw him aside, taking
the chain and the knife in different directions at
his destination, but Rey, with the advantage of his
agility, took the knife again and like an injured feline,
jumped to the the back of Kraw who, when trying
to hold him, found himself immobilized with the
knife in his neck; dominated, without more force,
with the knife to the neck, he chose to surrender and
again there in the room Rey returned to rule and was
accepted into the gang; he had passed the test.

None of the previous combatants had got to defeat
that human mass, however, before Rey's ability,
Kraw, the exhibition mass, had been subjected:

---- Enough, it is enough; Welcome, it will be nice
to have a warrior like you reinforcing our block. ---
Katiburo said.

---- Thank you for welcoming me as one of you, that
there is no prejudice, okay? ---- Rey asked.

--- Of course yes; Katiburo already pronounced it,
so welcome. --- Kurt said.

Everyone approached Rey to shake his hand with pride, including Kent and Kraw, then everyone returned to the round tables where they chose to celebrate Rey's acceptance; Katiburo went to the bar from where he took a bottle and some crystal glasses, which he brought to the table where they were; the bartender brought ice, and they toasted the rock for an eternal encounter:

--- Cheers, and fellowship. Katiburo said.

They clinked glasses and spilled a bottle of wine on Rey's head.

VI

Not always the force

can more than reason.

A few days passed before Mr. Alfonso arrived from his trip, and at the moment when they were precisely trying to define the circumstances in which the meeting with Tom had taken place, instantly and unexpectedly, the lord of the house, Martha's husband, and father of the girls made an appearance.

Mr. Alfonso, accompanied by Adolfo, who has been a regular pretender of his daughter, Candileja, and who, even without lacking the father's approval, has lacked the disposition of his daughter, Candileja; When he arrived, while Adolfo was in the car arranging the business documentation, his protégé from Candileja, he goes directly to the residency, but upon entering, Adolfo's reaction is one of surprise:

--- Good afternoon… oh, I see that we have a visitor. --- He said with some intention.

--- He is Adolfo — Says Ana Casilda introducing Adolfo with Tom.

---- Hello, nice to meet you, I am known as Tom! --- Tom says holding out his hand, but he realizes that Adolfo has left it extended.

---- It's a pleasure. --- Adolfo answered but without corresponding to the hand that Tom had extended to him. --- Candileja, I would like to talk to you. --- He said.

Candileja who has seen Adolfo's attitude towards Tom, comes with a negative:

--- I don't think we have anything to talk about. --- Candileja said.

---- Oh, so like this? Okay. --- He said as he walked out again, slamming the door behind him.

---- Don't listen to him, he's rude; I'm sure he's going to gossip with dad but I don't care.

A moment later Mr. Alfonso entered and addressed Tom, without giving time for an explanation.

--- Excuse me, I don't know who you are but I'd rather you leave us alone; I have something to deal with my family --- Mr. Alfonso said to Tom.

 ---- Alfonso! ---- Martha expressed astonished at the irruption of her husband.

---- Shut up, Martha. --- Alfonso replied radically.

Tom, a little confused, exchanged a look with Candileja again, and justifying himself before Ana Casilda said:

---- I'm fine now; don't worry about me, talk to your father, I'll call later to tell Robert where I'm staying; keep the motorcycle for me and when I can drive it again, I'll pick it up; It has been a great pleasure, see you soon, and thank you very much.

He left the place, but not before fixing a deep look at Adolfo who had remained at the exit.

Tom walked away and went in the direction of Manolo's house.

Candileja had a great dilemma; Mr. Alfonso, her father, intended to marry her to Adolfo, but on the contrary, she thought that her meeting with Tom was the opportunity that she had waited for so long time and felt that this opportunity was a happiness that, due to coincidence of destiny, had come into her life and she did not aspire to let her pass, so she chose to follow and ran after him, due to the speed of the rush, Adolfo, who was still at the door, was forced to step aside to give way without being hurt.

--- Candileja, come back, I want to talk to you, where are you going? --- Mr. Alfonso exclaimed without being obeyed.

He looked at Martha and Ana Casilda inquisitively suggesting an answer.

--- I wanted to explain but you didn't let me, and now what can we do? Tom is Robert's brother, he was injured trying to save Candileja and we had him here waiting for him to heal, and now look what you did. --- Martha explained.

---- So is dad; we have to apologize to him, that is now what Candileja is trying to do. --- Ana Casilda added.

Due to the unexpected information, Mr. Alfonso, feeling upset, decided to retire somewhat stunned to his rooms.

--- I'm sorry Adolfo, I'm not feeling well, I'm going to rest, see you tomorrow. --- Said.

---- Good afternoon, it is still early but the body warns; I'm leaving too, see you soon. --- Adolfo said.

---- Bye for now, Adolfo. --- Martha said, while Ana Casilda just waved her hand to say goodbye.

Adolfo withdrew while they, seeing him leave, gave each other a look of complicity, hugged each other and entered Ana Casilda's room.

Candileja was still after Tom until she managed to catch up with him:

--- Tom, Tom; wait…

When he turned and saw Candileja behind him, Tom experienced a feeling of relief and smiling said:

---- what are you doing! Why have you been following me? How may I help you? --- Asked.

---- Throughout; forgive me, I didn't want to let you go without giving you an explanation; My father wants to make me marry that scoundrel, but I don't want him, I'm sorry for the misunderstanding.
--- Said Candileja. Tom looked into her eyes and discovered that a spark of interest emanated from her concern of that should be reciprocated by him:

--- You don't have to worry; I understand the situation; Thanks for worrying about me --- Tom replied with some tenderness.

--- Thanks to you --- she replied, corresponding to the manifestation that Tom had just expressed, and added --- what are you planning to do?

--- When I am healthy, I will look for a job, but first I will look for Robert; Maybe he can help me, for now I'm going to Manolo, he lives in Altamirano County. --- Tom said.

---- I don't see it bad; but for now, you will not be able to work with that wound. --- Candileja replied.

---- I'll do my best--- Tom insisted.

---- You have to get cured again… Ah, I know, I think that on that side everything will be resolved, we will go to Angel Luis, he is a cousin of us who is almost receiving a doctor's degree; he will be able to heal you and possibly even let you host you.

---- I appreciate everything you have done, but you don't need to bother --- Tom said with a certain ceremony.

---- It is not a bother ... I will help you whether you want it or not. --- Candileja said decisively.

---- Well; it's okay, I'm so happy that I'm not bursting with joy because my skin is hard. --- Tom added, while he felt invaded by a peace and enthusiasm never experienced. Instead, Candileja smiled determined to carry out everything she had decided:

---- Ah, it seems that Robert called, they notified the clinic that he will be absent for three days, we had not been able to establish contact because he left the cell phone in the office, while you were resting Dr. Olmedo gave us those details, we had not had time to talk to you about that, but as soon as he communicates, we will inform him that you are here and we will go looking for you.----Said.

He put her hand into the small pocket and took a one-hundred-dollar bill and, extending it to him she added --- This is for you to help yourself, in case you need something, until we resolve the matter of your accommodation. --- Candileja expressed.

Tom was embarrased to accept the money and said:

--- Thank you, that is not necessary; I think I have a sufficient amount to sustain myself economically for the necessary time. ---replied

Then Candileja without insisting, took the money and unexpectedly deposited it in the pocket of the orange shirt that he was wearing while saying:

--- You don't have to be embarrased, for me you are already family, nothing is casual in life, use that money, soon, everything will be solved, let me take you wherever you go, which is better than doing the tour walking; wait a minute, I'll bring the car. --- Said.

Tom, faced with the reality generated and the persuasive act of Candileja, accepted the proposal without further ado; So he went back to her and waited for her to take the vehicle out and when she went to Tom she was accompanied by Ana Casilda, who also took the opportunity to apologize to Tom and they left to drop him off at his destination.

It had been 20 minutes before they arrived where the practitioner cousin Angel Luis, they parked and while, Ana Casilda went to the door where she rang a bell that sounded like a police whistle and a few minutes later Angel Luis appeared at the door, and with a ceremony of confusion he greeted his cousin effusively, accompanying her back to the car opening the door of the back seat where Ana Casilda was, and inviting they to come in, they all went to the house; Angel Luis was older than everyone, although his age was not over 32.

Inside, instrumental music could be heard, the "Blue Danube" sounded in a burst of inspiration Angel Luis Surprisingly took Ana Casilda by the hand and made as if she were going to dance, everyone laughed:

---- Take a seat, how happy your visit makes me cousins, and you friend …

---- Tom. --- Said.

---- Yes, Tom, nice to meet you, I am Angel Luis, you are welcome, you are at your house.

---- Thank you. --- Tom replied.

---- Okay, then cousins, what can I offer you, juice, beer? I don't offer you tequila or cognac because you get hot for me, hahahahaha.

---- Give me a beer. --- Ana Casilda said.

--- I want orange juice, if you have. --- Candileja said.

--- Ah, don't worry, I'm stocked, and… what do we give Tom…? --- Angel Luis asked.

---- I prefer water, as you can see, I am medicated. ---- Tom said.

----- Sure, what happened there?

---- That is precisely what we come to but serve us and then we will tell you. ---- Candileja said.

---- Sure, sure. ---Angel Luis said.

After they had tasted the drinks, they told Angel Luis everything that had happened with luxurious details, and he showed that he was very willing to serve. He took advantage of the visit to clean it and replace the bandage; He offered him the accommodation that had been requested for him, however, without ceasing to thank him, Tom preferred to go back to his friends who did not know everything that had happened since the day of the altercation, and to whom he wanted to give an explanation.

Then Angel Luis left him a schedule so that he could go to heal while he was affected; After saying goodbye, Ana Casilda and Candileja directed him to Manolo's house as he had requested, and then they returned. Since that day, communication between them had been consolidated.

VII

When the light shines

the heart is ennobled.

Some days had passed and Adolfo had not trying to speak to Candileja again, until one morning while Candileja was reading the press; She heard the phone ringing, she let it ring until the call was closed, but he dialed again, after Candileja explored some pages of the newspaper, and noticing the insistence, she found herself motivated and standing up, answered the phone:

---- Hello. --- Candileja replied.

When he heard her voice, on the other side he hung up the phone, Adolfo only was looking for a way to know if Candileja was at home.

---- Uh, they hung up, who could it be? ... well, surely some funny guy.

Then Candileja put the phone back on its pedestal and continued reading the newspaper, twenty minutes later the doorbell rang. Candileja walked to the door with newspaper in hand:

---- Who is it? --- she asked.

---- It's me, Adolfo, Candileja, may I come in? ---- answered him.

---- What do you want? Adolfo. Candileja questioned.

---- I have come to look for something that was forgotten the last time I was here. --- Said he cunningly.

Candileja opened the door and he came in abruptly, rethinking his intention:

----- What isthis, Adolfo? ---- Candileja questioned again.

---- I want to talk to you. --- Adolfo said decidedly

---- I had already told you that there is nothing to talk about, what do you intend to propose me? ---- Candileja answered.

Faced with that attitude, Adolfo felt somewhat disappointed by which she questioned sharply:

---- Where are the elders here? --- Adolfo asked in an authoritative tone.

---- They are not here, tell me, what really you want to deal with me? --- Candileja questioned again.

---- Today I beg you again to love me; I want you to be my wife, our families are well positioned and well off, we will always have everything, we will lack nothing. --- Said him with macabre intention.

---- And I, again, I beg you to leave me alone; Don't bother me. ---- She replied, sure of what she wanted.

Faced with that attitude, Adolfo prowled around while gesturing lightly until he placed himself in front of her, staring at her, he warned her:

---- "A monkey in silk is a monkey no less", you will be my wife even if you don't want to. --- He said.

---- Take your hands off me gross, you're hurting me, get out and don't bother me anymore. ---- She told him, breaking free of his tentacular claws as she slapped him.

Adolfo, rubbing the side of his face where he received the slap, warned with the greatest courage:

 ---- Okay, I'm leaving; but I assure you that you will pay it to me, and you will do it as you cannot imagine. ---Adolfo Said, as he came out pulling the door roughly.

Disgusted and without thinking, he did not waste time and without preamble he went to the Dragon's tavern, where he went with a crude intention; he sat at a lonely table where he realized that a euphoria invaded him, then he discovered that Katiburo was looking at him, and through a sign he indicated that he should come closer.

Following that call, Katiburo approached:

---- Sit down Katiburo, I have to talk to you. ---Adolfo Said.

Katiburo sat down, lit a cigarette, and ordered a beer

from the bartender.

---- How do you want to talk to me? ---Katiburo asked.

---- I have a job for you… Do you remember Mr. Alfonso? The girl's father, the one I told you about, the one I'm in love with. --- Adolfo Affirmed.

---- Oh, yes, that bourgeoisie, how not to remember him? and more if he has money. --- Katiburo said.

---- Yes, the little job this time is about him… I want you to kidnap him and force him to sign a will where he leaves me all his fortune; In exchange I will have some hard dollars for you --- Adolfo said.

---- And where can we locate him? --- Katiburo questioned.

---- It is very easy, as he is not at home, nor in the company it is certain that he is on the farm, but the best thing is that you call me; I will tell you for sure where to find him, be aware, I will go to confirm if he really is on the farm; if so, when he returns, you will be able to fall on him.----He said with irony.

He took out a notebook from his jacket, jotted down an unnamed phone number, then tore out the page and put the written number in Katiburo's possession.

----- Well, then what will you do? ---- Katiburo questioned.

---- Call me at the time that is on the paper and get ready for today. ---- Adolfo clarified solemnly.

He said goodbye and cautiously left the place; Meanwhile, Katiburo dedicated himself to motivating his team of criminals; who did not hesitate to rejoice at their leader's report. On the other hand, two hours later, Adolfo had already put his plan to work, he had prepared the document where Mr. Alfonso should deposit the signature; he put it in a briefcase, and chose to play the thief trying to obtain the sum that he had forged to subtract from the safe of his father, it was the amount he would have to pay. He entered his father's private office, removed a painting that covered the safe, and using the memorized combination proceeded to open the safe. Right at the moment of activating, the telephone was heard ringing; He took the receiver and without waiting he answered the phone call:

---- I can hear you from this side, tell me to see who's talking ... ah, you're Katiburo very good; I'm preparing what was agreed… yes, okay, we'll get together in plaza de la opera, as usual, yes at five, it's fine until later, bye. ---He said saying goodbye, and hanging up the receiver.

Adolfo had mounted his plan, and was polishing it, he was giving it the last brushstrokes, the blindness of his unconsciousness was leading him to ruin the lives of those he pretended to love, he could not accept Candileja's rejection, so he had thought that betrayal as revenge, would be the best way to balance his ego.

He concluded the subtraction he had started, counting a few bundles of hundred-dollar bills until his account reached five thousand:

---- I don't think Dad will be angry because I invested these five thousand on my own to pay the boys; I will return them soon. ---- He said thinking aloud; As he finished putting the money in the briefcase, rang the doorbell:

---- Hell, they almost found me. --- He thought.

He went to open the door, but when he looked, he

discovered that Rey was waiting for him; by the way he dressed he did not hesitate to identify his origin gently from him. ---- Hello man, are you by any chance the one called Adolfo? --- Rey questioned with an outsider accent.

Yes, in this moment outside of you, there is no other here that responds to that name; and you show me that you are new among cats; He affirmed that with ease and without flinching.

---- That's right, but how do you know I'm one of the cats? --- Rey questioned.

---- for your clothes, only cats wear it. --- Adolfo claimed.

---- Ah, yes, because of the clothes… I'm wearing it and even so, I don't realize that this identifies me… Can I come in? --- Rey said.

Oh?… it is not necessary; I was going to go out. --- Adolfo said blocking the door.

---- That's why I'm here, Katiburo asked me to accompany you. ---- Rey said.

---- Well, if that's the case, let's go. --- He said with determination.

He seized the briefcase he had packed, and they left.

Adolfo got on the back of Rey's motorcycle, and they went to the agreed direction, however just as they left the place, Juvenal, Adolfo's father, was driving his sports car, very capable of impressing, he parked and got out of the car, and with his briefcase entered the main room. Really Juvenal was that widower who lived next to his spoiled son; Adolfo was the only one and very dear to him; inside the house he wandered and discovered that there was no one.

----- How strange that he is not, I thought that Adolfo had already returned. --- Juvenal muttered between his teeth---- Well, surely he has entertained himself with friends.

He leaned back on a beautiful dark brown leather cabinet and found comfort massaging the battered body he carried; He lit a cigarette and while he was smoking, he opened the briefcase he brought with him, took four packs of bills, and gazed at him in silence; He went to the safe where he intended to deposit it, however he felt a chill invade him, when he discovered that the painting that had long been covering the safe was no longer in place.

Adolfo had forgotten to return it to its place when he had seized the money; Juvenal had been drastically disturbed, much more when he discovered that a large sum of money was missing, then armed with patience, Juvenal Confessed to himself --- It can't be--- He reflected silently--- No, Adolfo wouldn't dare to make such a move; Whenever he has needed something he has asked me, why should he do it now?… But only he and I, we know the combination of the box… Well, I will deposit these and ask him about the other money… what is he up to now?

As he thinks he does, and he organized the money inside the box and decided to leave again.

VIII

The voice of conscience

balances justice

Upon his return from the farm, Alfonso realized that a checkpoint mounted by the cats was stopping him, right at a very little-traveled intersection surrounded by trees, they had set up an ambush, as had been agreed between the cats and Adolfo. The traffic appeared blocked, they had placed logs and crossed the motorcycles in the center, forcing him to stop, while the criminals remained hidden, entrenched like guerrillas in battle; Alfonso, a few scared and surprised at the same time, got out of the car, trying to mobilize logs, motorcycles and branches, while his observers came out of hiding.

They had covered their faces with scarves, while they fell on him with remarkable energies, so they pointed them at him, a revolver was placed at his temples, making him raise his hands:

---- Raise your hands, old rogue, put it up and do not try to do anything. --- Rey said, with a certain mischief.

---- What is it, are you not thinking of hurting me? ---- Mr. Alfonso replied.

---- No, of course not, nothing will happen to you, as long as you do what you are ordered to do. --- Rey replied.

---- Tell me, what do you want from me? --- Mr. Alfonso questioned with some concern.

---- Oh, no, almost nothing; We just want your signature. --- Katiburo said.

---- My signature? … For what? --- Mr. Alfonso replied.

--- Your signature for this document. ---- Katiburo affirmed

showing the Mr. Alfonso testament, who, catching it between his fingers, and looking at his characters read it with great interest.

While he read, Rey kept pointing a Colt 45 revolver at him; Suddenly begins to get dark, an atmospheric change precipitated and it was seven at night, the gang members turned on the lights of the motorcycles that were kept off, the moon began to rise in the depth of the sky; the night increasingly agitated the silence of the deserted road. Mr. Alfonso had managed to understand what they wanted to make him sign, he had filled himself with a surprising resentment, he did not believe how changing the human mind turned out to be.

---- But how do you think I'm going to sign something that hurts me? I can't believe that a stranger is aspiring to my fortune. --- He said with some determination.

---- I don't think I'm a stranger to you; the heir to this document. ---- Katiburo affirmed.

---- So… You mean what? …

Mr. Alfonso tried to find an answer, suddenly he felt interrupted, the presence of Adolfo, filled him with surprise and hope:

---- Yes, Mr. Alfonso, it means that I am behind everything--- Adolfo affirmed with a certain pinch of impudence.

--- What, you? … I can't believe that you have
Involved yourself in this with such shamelessness!
… Why? Do you think that I will hand over to you
the heritage I have for the future of my family?
even when you are an only child and will inherit
everything from your father! I do not understand
what you are looking for with this! Did you not
think the consequence of this thoughtless action?
---- Mr. Alfonso questioned.

---- I have thought about it very well, and I have
consciously decided it. ---- Adolfo affirmed,
unperturbed in his attitude.

---- I have treated you like a son, I have supported
you as a member of my family, and you see how
you pay me, I never thought that you were such a
scoundrel and blackmailer. --- Mr. Alfonso added
indignantly.

--- The fault of this is only your daughter; She is the
culprit of everything, and therefore, the one that
induced me to make this determination. --- Rodolfo
argued.

---- Sign soon stubborn old man, we are wasting

time and it is already dark. ---- Rey expressed, with some impudence.

---- You are a group of childs, (7) spoiled, and disrespectful influenced by the culture of robbery, before signing I prefer death. ---- Mr. Alfonso said.

(7) niños

Possessed by the momentum of rebellion; and reacting defensively, he tried to grasp a revolver that he carried at his waist and covered with his jacket, but he did not have time, Rey instantly shot him twice, leaving him lifeless, Adolfo still carried the briefcase in his hands, had been filled with fury and surprise and reproached with integrity:

---- Scoundrel, what did you do? You have spoiled everything, now if you think you are going to receive the agreed money, you are very wrong, so do not even dream about it.--- he said, He said, while trying to flee.

That action induced Rey, turned into a bloody assassin, to shoot him, leaving him seriously wounded. The night cried out for corpses and Rey, had been imbued in instilling terror:

----- Let's go before the police arrive. ----- Rey said, but, while they tried to retreat, Adolfo stood up, firing his revolver at any point and introduced a bullet into Kraw's temples. When Rey realized that Adolfo was still alive, full of courage, revolvers in hand, fingers on the triggers like a war in the old, West and how if they were competing for a precious trophy, Rey and Kent fired in a nervous breakdown:

---- Die, viper --- Rey said with resentment.

In the surroundings not far from there, the road patrol that heard the shots, used the radio and reported the shooting, while heading to the scene of the massacre, called for reinforcements; he had put on the siren that announced his presence in the surroundings, and soon other reinforcements joined in, when they heard the sirens of the patrol cars, the gang members mounted their motorcycles like junkies from the racetrack ready to ride; In less than five minutes, the gang was found with a locator Radar from the reinforcement units and through the loudspeaker the police officers warned:

---- We are the police, stop or we will be forced to shoot. ---- Announced the Sergeant of the patrol.

That expression seemed to Rey more than a

warning, a great challenge and without further ado, as the lord of violence, maddened and thoughtless, disobeying the order, started a shooting, firing in all directions, being supported by his companions, the police did not flinch in confronting them, on that occasion they freely resorted to magnum 357, and machine guns, they took cover with the patrol cars and returned fire; Kent was injured in the encounter; what Katiburo, Kurt, and Rey took advantage of to escape; the wounded, unable to move, were easy prey for arrest.

The reinforcements had arrived on time, the fire lasted a long time, and Katiburo, Kurt and Rey, who had seized the money, directed their motorcycles through the thicket, moving covered by the shadows of the night and the great treetops; They managed to escape, when a helicopter tried to fly over the area, they had disappeared.

The Sergeant called an ambulance and behind the ambulance a lieutenant and a corporal appeared, leading to the scene of the shooting, they were after the ambulance, the sirens competed.

Kent, had been taken to the central hospital from where he would be transferred to the prison of the inspector major, where they would find a way to make him confess before being tried.

The corpses of Adolfo and Mr. Alfonso had been taken to the morgue where the relatives were expected to attend, who would define identity; At the beginning speculations arose where some believed that it was account adjustment and others commented that it could be the work of the mafia,

But the less credulous made conjectures and tried to involve the fact with the vandalism of drug traffickers, due to the narco-dollar disputes, until that the prosecution ruled out any kind of relationship with the aforementioned topics.

when Robert found out that Tom was around, he looked for a way to communicate, however when he went to Manolo's residence with Ana Casilda and Candileja, he discovered that he was no longer there, the house was closed.

During the time that Tom had entered the West Point Academy, both brothers were forced to abandon their mother in the state of Washington, to fulfill their destiny; Robert had moved to Chicago and having lost communication links, they only found out what Mrs Bertha, a widow and single mother, told one and the other, when she managed to establish contact with her children.

Tom had devoted himself to a military career from a very young age, specializing in private investigation and upon graduation, he was assigned as a special agent of the secret service, and later he had received the covert mission, to infiltrate and capture, the representatives of the most feared gangs in Los Angeles California, where he and You, his mission partner, had been introduced with Rey, a feared

Gang of that state, and related to Chicago gang members, the agents did not hesitate to pass themselves off as other gang members, which would help them convince Rey to introduce them to the heads of some Chicago gangs, where they would develop their next mission.

Once the arrangements were made, they moved to Chicago at the time, which despite not being one of the American cities called to compete with other cities of lights, such as Las Vegas, or Paris in Europe, used to attract many criminals related to the underworld.

The pillars of drug trafficking had decided to hire young gang members to take them to venture into the distribution of narcotics in schools and universities, and the entire urban area combined in the four cardinal points had been very wisely distributed, which is why the federal government opted for infiltrate youth trained among

Gang who were now involved in arms trafficking to Mexico.

As we had said, Rey, who had been observed for some time in his functions, in Los Angeles, would be the best way to lead them to where the ringleaders were, and although he never knew that Tom, Manolo and You were undercover agents, before realizing it due to their criminal feelings, he had decided to defect and now he had become a dangerous rival who could throw all the progress made in the investigation to the ground, so it was urgent to remove him from circulation , at the most appropriate moment, so they had decided to face him.

He was the reason why when they returned to where Manolo lived, Robert, Ana Casilda and Candileja had not been able to find them; they would be keeping an eye on the cats that had been hired by the foxes, a gang run by the mafia that had been leading the exchange of drugs for firearms on the Mexican American border.

They had met in a border canteen located on the border of the strip that divided the passage between the two countries and between smoke, music and beer, the details were implementated, and there the negotiators from both sides were meeting, four from the Mexican side, the cats that accompanied Petroniny Gamboa, and Manolo, You and Tom as undercover agents who were dedicated to performing their various tasks, so while Tom dressed as a waiter had been dedicated to recording the conversation with a hidden device under the assigned table.

 You recorded with a hidden camera, and Manolo, disguised, played a parishioner who consumed; on the other hand, Petroniny Gamboa, special envoy of the Benbenuty family; He was a tall and stocky man, he wore a black jacket and gray pants, he was accompanied by the cats, in the people of Rey, Katiburo, and Pesuña, a recognized criminal of the Fox gang in the region.

They were there because they had been commissioned to negotiate a delicate order, which included two dozen ruger sp-101, plus 18 pieces of ruger kp 89; three dozen combined 357 magnum revolvers and semiautomatic 9mm Kel-Tec pistols, and alongside that 100-piece semiautomatic style AR-15 machine guns; 150 fifty bulletproof vests, 50 cartridge belt and one hundred grenades.

As readers will realize, that request was a whole arsenal, it was as if they had been preparing for the start of a war, and the truth was that they were not far from that situation.

Those who gave their faces in front of that request were no more than those in charge of purchasing the Durango cartel who had already programmed to unleash a wave of violence and kidnappings of influential citizens, in order to fulfill a mandate of more than five of the Bankers of the world, and two presidents of Armories that financed at the same time, the different sides in conflicts.

The purpose was to raise, overthrow, infiltrate and manipulate rulers in the world, with the aim of imposing a sovereign, who according to their beliefs, could satisfy the ambitions of their egos.

We really lived in a limited world, where everyone in their quest for earthly glories enslaved themselves to matter, however, you did not know, or rather you wanted to ignore that nobody could do more than what they were called to develop, even when forced free will in a banal competition.

The four buyers on the Mexican side were Police Colonel Aquilino Cortez; Lieutenant Germosen Aguilera; Sergeant Ezequiel Compres and Corporal Crispin Mendoza; The negotiation was for an amount of two million dollars, of which five hundred thousand would be advanced; and the rest would be paid at the time of delivery.

The 21st century would give rise to the revelation of a large part of the macabre projects that the dark sectors of humanity had hidden, at this time all those erroneous predictions that terrorized humanity. Terrorized humanity would be retracted, with the supposed destruction of the world, both held by some religious sects and the interpretation of a calendar attributed to the Mayas where they had given as a fact that on December 21, 2012, the world would end.

However, although none of this happened as many came to believe, the biblical symbolisms of the evolution and destiny of humanity would be deciphered. The world was heading for a fight of all against all; the 666 prophecy or what is the same, the so-called mark of the beast the apocalyptic prophecy was glimpsed in the plans of the Illuminati, to create and increase violence in order to promote global imbalance with the intention of imposing the pre-design of their whims. Now the envoys, as isolated pieces of purpose, managed to acquire the weapons of terror.

It had been commented that in later years, fatalities from firearms in the United States would exceed deaths from traffic accidents which at that time had suffered a drop of 22 percent, and instead deaths from firearms they had increased relative to their low level in previous years.

Based on the average trend over a ten-year period, between 2015 and 2025, gun deaths would increase to almost 33 percent, while those of traffic accidents would be reduced to 32 percent. According to specialists, the change would be attributed to public policies, such as the strictest vehicle regulations, restrictions on young drivers and a host of new security laws.

In relation to violence, at that time the Boston Ripper was already a forgotten chronicle, as was the Central Park murderer. Now the press reported various cases, among them the massacre of approximately 27 victims riddled with firearms perpetrated by Adam Lanza, over speckled like Newton's murderer, who by those days had killed his mother and about twenty children between the ages of six and seven, plus six women who had tried to protect him in elementary school Sandy Hook, in Connecticut: later becoming the 28th victim in a self-committing suicide. At that time, some relatives of victims who had died with the use of firearms believed they felt secure in possessing one for their defense.

Meanwhile the international community clamored for an authentic control of arms possession, such as one that had been implemented in Australia, which after a massacre perpetrated in Port Arthur, Tasmania, starring by Martin Bryant, who armed with a Cort Art-15 semiautomatic rifle, had perpetrated such a horrible act. He had distracted everyone's attention and by the time he was arrested, he had killed 35 people and injured 23, generating an unsustainable reaction, which led to a national debate in the Australian nation that motivates to emergency legislation. All that had resulted in a control of possession, having prohibited the sale of rifles and semi-automatic shotguns including assault weapons, and also prohibiting imports and possessions, declaring all those who ignored this law as criminals, for carrying weapons illegally.

Thus, the current rulers had increased a massive purchase of all existing weapons at that time, at a price of ten percent more than what had been sold to the public. In this way, it became impossible to repair it or sell it to black market mercenaries, and this program destroyed around 650,000 weapons of this type, dealing a strong blow not only to the manufacturers of weapons, but also to those who championed violence. anywhere in the world they used to feed on human pain.

 Now in America steps were being taken for something similar, however the National Rifle Association tried to justify the condition of its associates through some press conferences after the terrible Newton massacre. Precisely in the midst of the terrible scandal that the registry of mentally ill patients had disappeared from the database for arms sales, adding to all this, the clandestine sale at that time was being aired among the mafia, thugs and gang members; and although the violence continued to envelop the land, nations that produces arms did not want to give their arm to twist.

At that moment Tom, in his waiter costume, with a false mustache, was approaching the negotiating table:

---- Something to drink? --- He questioned.

---- Yes, please bring a bottle of brandy with lemon and a snack. (8) ---- Colonel Aquilino Cortez went ahead to say, Tom looked Katiburo in the eye, as if he were asking him the same question and he, having understood it, also replied:

(8) refers to a snack of cookies, ham and chopped cheese.

---- Yes, the same for everyone. He said.

---- Tom withdrew in silence, while Rey, who had the question of where she had seen him before, commented:

---- I have the impression that I have seen that waiter, but I do not remember where I know him from --- He Externalized.

---- Rey, Rey, don't start imagining things, this is the border and we come from Chicago, from there to here there is a long way to go. --- Pesuña affirmed.

---- You may be right ---- Rey said somewhat convinced.

A few minutes later Tom returned with the order; He carefully served the table previously decorated with a tablecloth and integrated by the unification of others, taking an extension that allowed the eight diners to chat comfortably. Everything had gone perfectly without any altercations; Later, when everyone had left, Tom, You and Manolo, still in disguise, went up to the room on the second floor, which was the one they used as headquarters to comment on the progress made in that first meeting.

The recordings deciphered the point, time and day of delivery of the shipment that would take place shortly thereafter.

--- The truth is that with that mustache, you look like Pancho Villa. --- Manolo commented.

--- Yes, thank goodness it was like that, since Rey was about to recognize me, I thought there would be shots. --- Tom answered.

--- The important thing is that we left without being recognized. ---- You added.

---- That's right, there is nothing to worry about. --- Manolo said.

That night they got ready, after giving the report, they had dinner in the room; The next day they would return to Chicago, where the operation center was located and where they would go to make preparations for the day of delivery. At dawn, in their normal conditions, they traveled the route that would take them to Chicago. Some notifications had come in about the inappropriate use of weapons and this time they came from New York, where a gunman killed two firefighters who had tried to put out a fire that he had caused in his own home.

IX

Raise the spirit to the limits

of the soul, it is an act of consecration.

After the Sandy Hook massacre, the National Rifle Association had come under heavy pressure, and its representative at the time, Mr. Wayne la Pierre, who decided to break the silence on his first appearance, and was to urge the school authorities to maintain armed guards in all schools; However, he had been interrupted by the slogans and posters of activists who were demonstrating alluding to the fact that the National Rifle Association (NRA) was killing their children, and that before mentioned Association "had blood on its hands."

The debate on gun control persisted, intensified every day; An international treaty was required to regulate the arms trade worldwide, and in this proposal the United Nations (UN) was at the forefront, who had voted in favor of reopening the negotiations.

On that topic, that they had been stagnant when the United States in its opposition had obstructed the talks, as an electoral strategy, during the re-election of President Barack Obama, which at that time in the 21st century, was the month of July 2012, and under pressure from the opposition, he had led analysts to accuse him of giving in to pressure from Republicans, Congress and the National Rifle Association in an election year.

Not so long after other fatal crimes had passed when an ex-convict had seized the Bush master AR-15 semi-automatic rifle, with a 100-round drum magazine, with which he fired at Webster's firefighters, precisely the same model as he had used Adam Lanza, Newton's killer. All those misfortunes one after the other had reactivated the spirits of the international community, so that the recently hindered conversations were resumed, above of the strong obstruction of the (NRA) that was radically opposed to the lifting of any type of regulation against these weapons and their chargers, despite the continuous record that had been marking a horrendous trajectory of violence.

At that time there was talk of an alleged culprit in the Aurora massacre in Colorado, which had precisely occurred in July of that same year, 2012, and who was attributed, among other weapons, a Smith & Wesson AR-15, with a charger similar to the ones they had used in previous massacres. In other words, a 100-round magazine that exceeded a normal tubular in capacity; so the strong opposition of the National Rifle Association NRA was seen as impudent), whose radicalism had been so great that it had not only blocked gun laws, but was also proclaiming its effort to block an international treaty on the arms trade. Precisely the same treaty that they had previously blocked in the first months of that year 2012.   Therefore, the intention was to resume negotiations on March 23, 2013. What was understood was that there was proof that life gave, and they had to be assumed with humility, because man could not always rule his senses, much less bend his heart. If life wrappes us after the contradiction, we should not judge a good intention because after the pain, that disappointment also usually comes; By that time the influence of the NRA was so great that it had managed to impose a "checkmate" in its favor, because he had managed to paralyze the legislation with a letter. It was a letter that, as a subsistence emergency that the (NRA) had up its sleeve, and it was an openly declared opposition with the signature of 50 senators of the United States Congress, where the signature of eight of the Democrats who sustaining power stood out. They were seeking reelection, so they had been persuaded by Republicans and 130 members of the House of Representatives.

The truth was that the NRA, at that time, did not care about the fate of the weapons that it supported; so he was indifferent if those weapons went to countries subject to embargo, or if they were used for crimes against humanity, or war crimes or violation of international humanitarian law, or to create or promote violence in all its magnitudes. Amid all this confusion an author named Andrew Feinstein had alleged in his book: "The Shadow World: Inside Global Arms": " I have not seen anywhere else in the world a firearms lobby that has the level of influence that the NRA has over the government of USA."

To this added Andrew Feinstein, who in the recent past at the time had been a member of the African National Congress in the South African parliament: "The US buys and sells almost all weapons like the rest of the world all together, so what happens in the US is going to have a huge impact on the rest of the world."

The truth was that since those times of the Wild West that history records and that incidentally had inspired the Hollywood film industry, and the North American nation, had been called to evolve in violence, firearms had manifested as a value, as a stamp of the culture of several of the states that made up the Federation. The values established as cultural elements would not be lost overnight, so the proposal would have to be debated with all the splendor of the intellect, and both Tom, as Manolo and You, knew when starting their mission, not only that It was like plowing over the sea, but to solve that social problem that had spread throughout the world, it would have to be traced, as Gabriel Garcia Marquez put it, "a line in the sky".

It was as if before finding a permanent solution, the descendants of that generation had to start over, starting from scratch. While the undercover agents reflected on the mass murders that had occurred that same year, and commented on those places where the most painful crimes had been generated and as they were reviewing a troop, they mentioned several, among which they referred to:

Aurora, Colorado, the Sikh Temple in Wisconsin, and Sandy Hook Elementary School in Newton, Connecticut. Like the murder in Florida of a teenager called Trayvon Martin who had been attacked with a firearm, despite being unarmed; This generated a wave of protest where the police who had refused to arrest the perpetrator of the crime, was forced to act in order to put him under the custody of the authorities at that time, it was a man who was called George Zimmerman.

Thus upon arriving to Chicago, the undercover agents went to the meeting house; Manolo's lair, where they would return to their usual lives, to their motorcycles, and to their retrospective stories: so they commented on what they had experienced in the face of that operation.

---- Are you sure, that Rey did not recognize you? --- You questioned.

---- I don't think so, you know how he is, if he had recognized me, he would have made a scandal at that precise moment. --- Tom expressed

---- I think so ... I think Tom is right. --- Manolo clarified.

---- I hope so, he could pretend not to know you, and then act on his own, resorting to blackmail. --- You suggested.

Tom: --- The most important thing is not to trust. --- Tom emphasized.

--- We will take the appropriate measures. --- You said.

As they argued heatedly, the phone rang.

Manolo threw himself up to the second floor, and when he answered the phone, he discovered that on the other end of the line a female voice was asking for Tom:

---- Good afternoon, please, can you connect me with Tom? --- questioned the sweet voice on the other end of the receiver.

--- May I know who is looking for him? --- Manolo answered.

---- Yes, tell him please that Candileja is asking for him, and he will come. --- Candileja insisted.

---- Very well, wait a moment. --- Manolo said while leaving her on hold he approached the staircase shouting:

--- EE., Tom, someone wants to talk to you on the phone. --- Manolo said.

---- Who is it? --- He questioned as he walked to the second floor.

--- You will know who is it. --- Manolo said without telling him who it was, seeking to surprise him.

Four weeks had passed since Tom had seen Candileja; now she was calling him not only with the intention of communicating it with Robert, but also to make a proposal in relation to the statements supplied by Mr. Wayne el Pierre, about the armed guards inside the schools.

For her, education was the best way to claim; She believed that the virtue of knowledge was in reading, that it was something like working for the national future, to raise awareness for world peace, many times she used to think that when the time came for the light to shine, there would be a true balance for peace and serious social demand, the abolition of world violence.

---Hello, good afternoon, I anticipate my wishes that my friends be happy; Who am I talking to? --- He asked confidently.

---- The only ones of your friends who are sad are Robert and I, victims of the indifference of ignorance and pride that foster the vanities of this world, I know that ignorance is the blindness of the spirit, and that the wise is outraged, when the ignorant forget their duty because of the pridethat vanities provoke.

--- Candileja said with the intention of generating a reaction in Tom.

---- Candileja! How nice to hear you one more time; I know that my behavior is not worthy of your solidarity, forgive me, I owe you an explanation, but it must be personally. --- Tom replied patiently.

---- You don't have to give it to me, but to your brother who accompanied me to look for you and when we went, we didn't find you. --- Candileja said more calmly.

--- Oh, So did Robert come back? Good, tell me what time will we meet? --- Tom questioned.

---- Stay where you are, I'm going there--- Candilejas warned.

---- Well, fantastic, I'll wait for you here, see you later. ---- Tom replied, hanging up the receiver.

There was a moment of silence before Tom came downstairs again to inform his companions that he would be absent for a short time.

He quickly prepared himself so that when Candileja appeared he would not have to wait for him, because as he had planned it that way it happened and in less than half an hour the horn of Candileja was heard ringing in front of the house, he left quickly while saying goodbye with a gesture of camaraderie; Manolo and You were looking out the window until they saw him boarding Candileja's car, which received him very cordially with an affectionate kiss and immediately Tom boarded, started the car with some speed.

Half an hour later they were already at the Candileja's house where they would be running out of time for Robert and Ana Casilda to arrive.

How is it that, being able to explain everything to me from the first moment, you did not do it? at least you could call me and tell me that you would be absent, at least then I would have a convincing argument to explain to Robert, without passing the embarrassments that I have had that I have gone through with him. --- Said Candileja, while Tom looked for a way to justify himself.

--- Sorry, next time I will keep it in mind, I assure you that it will not happen again. --- Tom expressed convincingly.

---- It's fine, I'll trust your words. --- She affirmed with a persuaded girlish smile.

The room was divinely decorated, the carpet had been changed, and now it was noticeable with more details that it combined with the velvet furniture, in the background a tall brick-colored marble fireplace stood out, and in a corner, something like an armor of Don Quixote de la Mancha, which pointed to a door that led to a room where there were three shelves full of various books that formed a library.

They had additional seven minutes of conversation when Robert and Ana Casilda appeared at the front door, who when they saw Tom could not feign their joy, Robert advanced towards him and both merged in a surprising and emotional hug, which made it seem like the siblings, like uncontrollable crying children, suddenly those tears that are typical of family encounters were seen after many years.

--- Brother, it's nice to see you. --- Tom expressed lovingly.

---- I can not measure the joy, and the level of satisfaction that brings me to meet you again after five long years;

How have you been? --- Robert questioned, while he adhered it to his chest tenderly.

---- As absorbed as you; I excused your absence at my graduation, Mom explained to me that you were in a specialization internship and I could understand it, when I read about forensic pathology. --- Tom replied.

---- You are not going to tell me that in West Point in addition to military techniques they also taught you medicine. --- Robert questioned as they stopped embracing; while Tom went to greet Ana Casilda, who was still waiting to be greeted.

---- Hello Ana Casilda, how long? --- Tom said as he greeted her with a hug and a kiss on the cheek.

---- Tom, it's nice to know that you're fine, we were worried about you and we didn't know what to say to Robert, you left without leaving any traces.

---- Yes, I know, none of that will happen again; A job opportunity came up at the border and I left without giving me time to let him know, I'm sorry. --- Tom replied.

---- It's okay. ---- Ana Casilda replied.

After the euphoria calmed down and the moment of calm arrived.

---- When did you come back? --- Ana Casilda questioned.

---- Last night. --- Tom said.

---- Oh, you can't imagine how we missed you, Candileja was very distressed for being absent without telling her--- Ana Casilda said.

---- Yes, I know, she confessed it to me, while we were on our way here, I also want to offer you my most heartfelt condolences before the death of your

father, I knew that Adolfo was involved, I'm sorry.
--- Tom affirmed.

---- Thank you, it seems that he was destined to pass
away that way--- Ana Casilda affirmed.

---- I'm really sorry, but there are things that do not
depend on us. --- Tom answered.

--- That's right--- Ana Casilda affirmed.

At that moment Mrs. Martha appeared accompanied
by Rudy.

---- Oh, mother Martha, where were you?... I had
missed you--- He said as he greeted her with a
kiss on the cheek. --- And you Rudy, how are you?
---Robert asked.

---- I'm fine, brother-in-law, accompanying my mom.
---He said, while discovering Tom's presence, and
she got ready to greet him.--- Hello, Tom, it's good
that you came.---- Rudy said.

--- Hello, Rudy, and you Mrs. Martha, how have you
been? --- Tom said saluting.

---- Oh, my children here, waiting for the Lord to take me, my life without Alfonso does not mean anything --- Mrs. Martha affirmed.

----- Do not say that, when it is our turn we must all leave, but we must not anticipate the events of destiny. --- Tom affirmed.

----- That's right, Mom Martha, do not forget that you have all of us. ----- Robert said as he hugged her.

---- That's it, my children, if it were not for you, I don't know what my life would be like…. Well, stay there, while I retire to my rooms to see if I rest, I feel tired,

You are at home. ---- Mrs Martha said as she left.

---- Go ahead and don't worry, thank you very much.

Mrs Martha retired to her rooms while Rudy questioned:

--- Oh Tom, and where did you go? ---He asked.

--- Over there, over there, but I'm already here. — Tom affirmed.

--- Good, I want one of these days to lend me your motorcycle--- He affirmed.

---- Look young man, keep going, we have other things to talk about ---- Ana Casilda said.

---- It's okay sister, but don't be angry, I'll see you later. --- Rudy said as he continued in the same direction where a moment before his mother had gone.

Suddenly Robert admired, he stared at Tom, with a smile:

----- After my arrival I have been lucky to hear wonders about you, why don't you come to the patio with me so you can tell me better how all that was. --- Robert said, while he looked at Candileja and Ana Casilda with a certain camaraderie.

---- Oh, brother, maybe they are exaggerating, it was nothing important. --- Tom said, also elucidating a shy smile that Candileja let out, as he left the room hugging Robert. Ana Casilda and Candileja patiently followed him with their eyes while the brothers left the room.

---- And you, are you better, now that he's back? --- Ana Casilda questioned Candileja.

Her thin lips drew a slight smile on her angelic face:

---- Why not? Now more than ever I have no doubt that I love him. --- Candileja answered.

Ana Casilda took her by the arm and introduced her to her room where she could pay more attention to all the answers to so many questions.

That night the two couples dined out, first they went to a restaurant in the Altamirano neighborhood and after dinner they went in to watch the 8:30 show of a movie inspired by

The novel "The Tyrants of Paradise."

X

Humanity still breathes

vestiges of slavery

The next day Candileja's love was consecrated; Tom, had been pondered by Robert, in their previous conversation.

So the two brothers had stayed to sleep in the house of the loved ones but so that you, in your curious imagination, do not think more things than what really happened, I must warn you that they were all sleeping in separate rooms.

Later, in the early hours of the morning, almost at dawn, a strange and unexpected deluge began, whose gusts were furiously thrown towards the windows, creating a condition of thunder and lightning that scared Candileja, who, fearing to continue sleeping in solitude, chose for taking refuge in Ana Casilda's room.

Then Ana Casilda, getting up, went to the room where Robert slept, which was located on the second floor.

All being forced to receive the dawn where Robert had slept, including Tom, who upon hearing the movement in the second-floor corridor had chosen to open the door.

It was Saturday and throughout the day it had rained abundantly, and it seemed that it would not clear until the hour when the sun went down, since they had chosen to dedicate themselves to the game during their stay, so they played some games of chess where Candileja and Tom They were looking for a way to checkmate Ana Casilda and Robert, who imposed themselves on him, giving him more than one defeat.

At that moment Tom felt happy and understood that all this was still a way of smoothing down rough edges and removing the stresses of the hectic life, which at his young age had begun.

So, although he had not commented anything in relation to his mission, there was a moment when a surprise assailed him leaving him thoughtful, it was Candileja's comment about the proposal of Mr. Pierre, president of the Rifle Association, regarding that in the system schools armed security had to be accepted; from what Candileja had told him that it was time for the democracy that was so much advocated in America, began to become a reality.

He thought that the right thing to do was for the proposals to be consulted in a plebiscite with the associations of parents and friends of the school so that instead of the proposal of Mr. La Pierre, that consisted in an armed guard at the campuses, it would better install cameras in the classrooms whose central unit was monitored and supervised by a specialized security assigned for this purpose.

Candileja understood that in this way any anomaly within the teaching system could be controlled, where the studentscould not raise false testimonies to the teachers, nor could they abuse the other students.

Where in addition, the pedagogical quality of teaching in schools could be tested, and mainly where students were not giving an adequate result in academic performance; in such a way that, additionally, the services of those chambers will help to evaluate the academic quality of the teaching staff.

She thought that if both proposals were put to a vote among the parents of the association, the results would decree the decision.

Tom had thought when listening that speech, that Candileja was much more intelligent than she appeared, and they even stopped the game of chess to embark on the discussion of such a wise idea:

--- I do not know when such a brilliant idea occurred to you and I would like to congratulate you on that, also to tell you that I am proud that my double sister-in-law is doubly intelligent and ... --- Robert spoke, who could not continue when interrupted by Tom:

--- The one who is really triple proud is me; For the great life partner that fate has assigned me, you are fantastic, Candileja.

--- Tom said, as he assaulted her with a kiss on the mouth.

--- uuhuhuh, hey, do not eat cheese in front of the hungry, sister, we are all proud of you, and although we know that this proposal will have to be debated not only among the associations of parents and friends of the school, but also by the councilors or councilors, It would be like a fight of dignity against money, on top of that, we will support you in everything that is within our power. ---- Ana Casilda added while giving him a hug.

Candileja was moved and even wanted to cry, which Tom took advantage of to hold her in his arms.

---- Okay, my love, we are your family, we love you and the right thing is that we tell you what we think. --- Tom argued.

---- Thank you, it is not so bad but I feel happy, and that is the way in which I can momentarily express my joy, thank you again family. --- She said as if stuttering from the tears that, as she expressed, they boosted her joy.

After the emotional moment, Mrs. Martha appeared with a tray that carried sugar, coffee, milk, and a liquid chocolate with some cups, so that they could enjoy it more.

So after having the unexpected aperitif, they took the opportunity to thank Mrs. Martha for managing her, and for the dating decision that Candileja and Tom had decided.

---- Mom, thank you for this appropriate sweat for this cold and rainy day, but I also want to let you know that now Tom and I have engaged in courtship, and from now on he will have a new son at home. --- Candileja Argued.

---- Ah, that news is pleasant for me and I want to congratulate you, I hope you get along well, get married and give me many grandchildren. Mrs. Martha said.

--- Mom, please ... Thank you. --- Candileja answered kissing her mother on her cheek.

---- Thank you Mrs. Martha, for opening the door to enter your family, I will not disappoint you. --- Tom said, hugging Mrs. Martha.

---- After such emotional moment let's toast with another round of coffee. --- Ana Casilda said while they served coffee again for everyone.

---- I toast to my great family --- Robert said, while the cups clinked.

---- And Rudy, mom? --- Ana Casilda questioned.

---- Sleep like a little angel. --- Mrs. Martha answered.

---- Well, he misses it. --- Ana Casilda commented, while everyone laughs at the same time.

A flash of lightning illuminated the room again.

After consuming the toast between joy and lectures, Mrs. Martha picked up the tray and returned downstairs, while the group resumed the game of chess.

XI

Surrender to the spirit

it is the same as recovering the essence of being.

A few months had passed since that day, when he received a letter ordering him to reintegrate the brigade along with You and Manolo, to participate in the raid stipulated for the day of the delivery of the weapons.

He then remembered once that he tried to travel to Mexico, where he verified that expression that Balzac used to name referring to people who were part of the government anywhere in the world, where he expressed that "the bureaucracy was a giant managed by dwarfs.

After this expression, he had observed in silence and without complaint how the rulers used to violate the human and civil rights of ordinary citizens in the name of borders and immigration.

He knew that the application of international human rights standards was governed by the principles of universality and non-discrimination; enshrined in the first article of the declaration that said that all human beings were born free in dignity and rights. Where the duty of states was raised, whatever their political, economic or cultural systems, to promote and protect all human rights and fundamental freedoms, understanding that non-discrimination was a basic principle of human rights, enshrined in the charter from the United Nations.

For this reason it was illegal for women to be tortured, murdered and denied participation in public positions, as well as those who did not seem what the officials conceived.

In the same way, it was illegal for states to allow officials to loot the public treasury of their respective countries, creating a kind of economic vacuum that expanded to its entire population, leading to forced immigration, which tended to force the economies of the countries to where the displaced decided to take refuge.

Well, at that time chaos and organized anarchy were expanding in the region, and the nationalist essence of the countries had been lost to globalization, money had become the flag of identification, at that time Mexico had already lost its essence of struggle like almost all the nations of the region, it had begun to subordinate itself to the dictates and whims of the northern neighbors who were exhibited as the owners of money, and therefore of political decisions; so it would be easy for him to buy and instruct the <<legislators>> of some Latin American congresses, the policy to follow, and violence had begun to be trafficked as a staple product.

This procedure had affected the youth of the entire region who only thought about branded products and to acquire them they spared no effort in getting involved in organized crime, in order to capture the resources that would allow them to fulfill their dreams of alienation and perversion.

Those same and many of them who, having learned and rehearsed great vices in the United States, there no longer being spaces for them in North American prisons, the government had chosen to deport them as remnants of chronic moral illnesses.

And those victimized perpetrators, without thinking about it further, in an effort to readjust to the forgotten limitations, came to spread the peace of the healthy, in their countries of origin, mainly in Latin America.

In this way, they created a kind of collective anxiety and phobia that tended to generate social violence, fostering imbalance and insecurity in community families, whether in the Dominican Republic, in

Mexico or El Salvador, in Colombia or Nicaragua or in those places of fragile ethical conduct whose corruption did not stop << not even at the door of the offices >> of their rulers.

All these conditions, at their extremes, were generating social envy, where a number of unconscious beings wanted to seize by force the properties that others exhibited.

At that time, the populations that waited for the responsibilities of the states to come into play looking for a way to stop these social scourges, many times used to be disappointed because many nations found it impossible because their main leaders had lost their moral quality.

with the patrimony with which collective wellnes could be developed, two or three used it to satisfy their personal egocentricities, and instead of investing it in their respective nations to educate and curb the social poverty of the population, preventing them from being motivated to murder. steal to eat or use imported vices; They took it out of the country to be stored in foreign banks.

And from a critical point of view, Tom thought that those sectors that did not care about the fate of their populations, were the same that had been infiltrated in all the governments of the world, obeying those scattered plans that the religious called "mark of the beast", whose supporters were very clear that everything would tend to be a kind of global slavery either through a debit card or a microchip mentioned.

Tom, still working in the service of the government of a power, understood that Iluminati and gray men aspired to impose a sovereign arising from among them; For this reason, the violence that spread throughout the world was not by chance; and, to achieve this purpose, they would first have to exterminate large masses.

All this contradiction generated great concern in him, who saw how in some Latin American nations, the poor who stole a chicken to eat often used to imprison him for ten years, and instead, the officials who looted the public treasury and robbed five and ten million, on the contrary, they paid him honors, decorated him and gave him amnesty.

He thought that although the world had fallen into a culture of depravity, it was necessary that measures of coercion and education be taken against corruption and crime as a prevention guideline, because without being pessimistic, he used to say:

<< The fight to the contrary brings us closer to the great conflict where there will be no solution, as long as there is no renewal in the spirit, and that will

not occur until the cycle of the wheel is completed, which will be when we return from zero. >>

Then the violence, and the Narco-industry had expanded their influence and the armories had an impact on the importation of sophisticated weapons that indirectly also contributed to the expansion of inclement violence, making it easy for the banditry industry to continue using Mexico as bridge to cross narcotics, among other possible smuggling.

All this problem had induced the governments of both sides to find themselves forced to undertake cooperative agreements, to combat that problem, which had led sectors of the Mexican government to act more as servile than loyal. But, in order for the reader to have a clear idea of what I am saying, let me tell you what happened with Tom:

Tom had always dreamed of visiting Mexico, many years before being involved in his love affairs with Candileja, then in his undercover role his identification had been changed, and he wanted to enter as a resident of the United States whom the immigration authorities they had withheld his original documents and denied American citizenship.

Although they had not stripped him of all his rights, he was somewhat limited, because he had been involved in a deportation process, endowing him with a document that at that time the immigration of North America nominated him:

"Form: 1-551" and that by the way before leaving New York, he wanted to verify if he would be valid in Mexico by visiting the Mexican consulate in New York, which would be the port of his departure.

For an instant Tom believed that everything would be resolved, but not, despite having obtained the authorization of the Border Department and the approval or consent of a Mexican consul in New York, and of his assistant, on behalf of both countries.

In addition to obtaining the approval of those who controlled the departure from New York to Mexico and having received a smile smeared with sadness from a Mexican who had checked his departure, at JFK Airport, representing the Aeromexico line for which he had been embarked.

What happened was, having flown for more than four hours, upon arriving at the Benito Juarez Airport, the immigration representatives in Mexico said they did not know the legal document that identified Tom.

And after questioning him with the certainty that Tom could be a dangerous entity, comparable in the mentality of those Mexican immigration officers, to a ponderous of the Drug Trafficking industry or to an explosive detonator of what in the United States used to call "Terrorists ", And his fear being more than his shame, they blocked his access to the Federal District, and after four hours of teasing and joking from the airport offices, they boarded him on a flight similar to the one that had taken him, returning him to New York , where they received him as the prodigal son, that rebellious boy who tried to give worries to their parents, escaping from home without warning.

Although nothing that had happened was Tom's fault, and despite the fact that he had claimed the return of the investment in the plane ticket, the Aeromexico line never reimbursed him.

Some people affected by violence with firearms had joined the campaign of non-violence and in different parts of the United States, he was seen raising banners protesting against this scourge.

XII

The ignorance,

it will always be a mother,

of all evils.

September 19 dawned sunny and cool, a soft and pleasant breeze blew through the atmosphere; It was the day that had been planned for the delivery in a place that had previously been the scene of more than one massacre of workers.

Two jets arrived first, one was gray and the other black; Kurt, El Pesuña, and some heavily armed men traveled in the black one, in the gray one Rey came and another group of men who were members of the fox gang; also as armed as the cats that also came in the black jeep, which together with the gray one would be doing a verification tour in the area, after exploring the surroundings, they returned to the meeting point; then they gave a brief information over the phone, in a loud voice and a few minutes later a long truck appeared with a long container in its structure a long container.

It also had the order bought inside, and it entered to an isolated and lonely highway that linked Mexico with the United States, an unknown point to coyotes and adventurers.

A helicopter flew behind it, carrying Mr. Petroniny Gamboa, representative of the Benvenuty family, accompanied by Katiburo and some personal bodyguards.

When they had already entered the no-man's-land area, a squad of the American military police appeared out of nowhere, including Tom, Manolo and You, who in their eagerness to act appropriately on behalf of the nation had made their greatest effort to dismantle that network of firearms traffickers forming a bloody shootout where at least five of the criminals had fallen.

However, some of the undercover agents had been exposed, since despite being disguised with the clothes that made him unrecognizable, due to those circumstances of fate, in the confusion of the rush, Manolo lost a piece of the disguise just when the vehicle occupied by Rey, was approaching the place where he was being exposed to the sight of Rey, who found it not difficult to recognize it:

--- I know who you are, if you are not a police officer you are an informant, all this will cost you dearly. --- Rey said, exposing the Personality of manolo, who felt upset at that imprudence.

--- If you already know, take care. --- Manolo replied in the midst of the confusion caused by the sharpened shots.

So much fuss was of no use, the truck managed to enter Mexican land with the load intact, there were some casualties on both sides and Petroniny Gamboa escaped from his pursuers who, because they did not contribute to the escalation of the sure scandal that would form, chose to return, leaving the mission uncovered and unable to prevent arms trafficking to Mexico.

A few weeks later, the scandal exploded, reaching repercussions and being the subject of debate between the authorities on both sides, but without the evidence being gathered to identify and punish those involved. In that case neither Colonel Aquilino Cortez, nor Lieutenant Germosen Aguilera nor Sergeant Ezequiel Compres, and much less Corporal Crispin Mendoza, who very diligently received the request that Petroniny Gamboa and his cliques had given them.

The weapons had ended up at the hands of the Durango cartel, for which reason an investigation had been initiated in the national territory that led to a series of murders and kidnappings that involved artists, politicians, police, among other sectors of Mexican society.

Then a war against drug cartels had been unleashed, led by the federal government of Mexico in cooperation with the United States, and in a few months in Guadalajara, the capital of the state of Jalisco, some official sources had reported the murder of five people. in events allegedly linked to organized crime; And later, the prosecution had located the bodies of three men, two of them had been beheaded, they had been found in the middle of a public road where they had been abandoned in plastic bags tied with adhesive tape, without the authorities being able to arrest any person linked to those facts. Great events were being generated linked to the violence, because in those same days in the town of Salto, the authorities continued to find corpses, and on that occasion, it had been a man that was approximately 30 years old he had been found dead in the trunk of his vehicle near the railroad track; he was blindfolded, and his head covered by a plastic bag.

The entry of those relatively clandestine weapons had begun to play a role of social outrage; in Guadalajara itself, on the outskirts of the metropolitan area, from inside one of the vehicles that had participated as reinforcement in the delivery of the weapons, a burst of eight shots had fired that hit the body of Corporal Crispin Mendoza.

He had managed to leave the scene of the crime, without anyone being able to obstruct the way of his escape, while Crispin Mendoza was torn between life and death.

Later, some police patrol cars appeared and followed by an ambulance, managed to pick him up on time and take him to the central hospital in Guadalajara, where, after having managed to get him out of harm's way, and be chosen as a witness for the prosecution.

Rey, who had now become a drug trafficking hit man, entered dressed as a policeman, and taking advantage of the changing of the guard, he entered his room where he using a pillow suffocated him, with no one showing up until after his death.

Rey had become quite a dangerous element for society; his evil had now crossed the border.

It was said that all that violence had been generated by a dispute held at that time by an organized crime group, which sought control of the area for the transfer of drugs to the United States.

Then among them it was said that Colonel Aquilino Cortez was one of the leaders of the powerful

Sinaloa cartel, that had generated divisions among some drug trafficking structures.

Los Caballeros Templarios, who were originally from Michoacan, were also mentioned as having tried to seize the municipalities in the border area between the two states, which had generated at least the deaths of a score of police officers and civilians killed in recent weeks that moment.

In any case, after the scandal, the raids had not stopped extending throughout the Latin American territory, reaching the north of Honduras, where an arsenal of weapons was seized, which included belts and saddles, an AK-47 rifle, armored clothing, among other objects, and in addition, five people who were guarding the raided properties were arrested and were being investigated.

All this was due to finding the whereabouts of the owners of the properties that were valued at five million dollars, when it was believed that they had dealt a severe blow to Drug trafficking, cataloged by the authorities as one of the causes of the high rates of violence in that country.

Back then, Before the alleged witnesses could give statements, they appeared strangled inside the cell without knowing who killed him. Violence had seized the outer reaches; security anywhere in the world was becoming a myth.

XIII

Patience is like

the drop of water, that

shed in assiduity

it subdues the matter it hits.

Five weeks had passed since the day of that dangerous raid and a Tuesday, during the month of August, at eight o'clock at night, and with You, Tom and Manolo, conferring on the development of events, they had been taken by surprise.

From a helicopter that was flying over the shelter that was serving as their headquarters near the border, they were suddenly shot at, several machine gun bursts preceded by a gasoline rinse alerted them to assume a defensive posture:

--- Hey, down, they're shooting at us. --- You expressed with all the eagerness of your soul.

--- We better get out; they are burning our cabin. --- Tom answered.

--- Take the camera and the computer. --- Manolo answered as he seized some binoculars that were in his wake.

To the gasoline, criminals had added a blaze of fire that in an instant ignited the cabin they inhabited, being able to remove only what was minimally necessary within the framework of the mission.

They managed to place the salvaged objects in the trunk of the car when suddenly they realized that the adventure was still continuing; They had been discovered, from the bushes four gigantic shadows were approaching them in a threatening way and they discovered that they were being pointed with two guns size forty-five and two machine guns.

--- How small is the world! Look who we meet, guys; record it. --- Rey said.

When they were investigated, they found on them in addition to their weapons of regulations, the identity plates.

--- Look Rey, we are dealing with policemen. --- Kurt exclaimed, while showing Manolo's badge.

--- I already guessed it, that's why we're here, Petroniny Gamboa will be happy to know that my assumptions were true. --- Rey argued.

---- What do we do? … Do we kill him? --- Cuervo asked.

---- Yes, man, we are going to kill him. --- Pesuña aded.

--- No, do not invent, remember that Petroniny wants you alive, and if we disobey him, we run the risk that we are the dead. --- Rey added, while reporting:

--- objective taken, we will move by land---he said through the radio.

---- Do you need a guard? --- Katiburo asked from the helicopter that was still flying in the vicinity.

--- Negative, everything is in control. --- He replied as they accommodated their prisoners in the gray car that was driving by the fourth of the men, he's called El Cuervo, and who also like Pesuña carried a machine gun, while Rey and Kurt continued pointing them menacingly with the forty-five pistols.

After accommodating the prisoners in the back seat, While Rey sat next to the chauffeur who was called to Cuevo, Kurt was going back in the door of the right side of the passenger as if blocking the access to You; Manolo was in the center, while Tom stood behind to Cuervo, the driver.

Close to the left door, Pesuña had positioned himself behind everyone, in the space used to place the suitcases, always pointing the machine gun at them.

The prisoners had been disarmed and held their hands up, while Rey's threat was on its way to materialize.

When the firefighters from the town closest to the place wanted to make an appearance, only the ashes remained.

Two police patrols from the area who had accompanied the firefighters, were able to discover the car that Tom, Manolo and You used to transport themselves and who by the way had remained there precisely by order of the executive command that had asked them to remain in that place from where it would be easier for him to enter and leave Mexico in order to clarify in greater detail the events that have already occurred in relation to arms trafficking.

Now Rey's threats had been carried out, and although the three had escaped the fire, the authorities already considered them missing; that same night the ten o'clock news reported on the tragedy where the disappearance of You, Manolo and Tom was emphasized, without their being identified as special agents of the government.

Robert, Ana Casilda and Candileja who were aware of Tom's mission, had begun to worry; But in order not to commit indiscretions, let's look at the topic that revolved the conversation of those who had precisely gathered to listen to the news:

--- Oh, something has happened and my heart tells me that although they are not dead they are in danger. --- Candileja said.

--- Calm down sister, we cannot anticipate events, Tom is trained to do his job--- Ana Casilda said.

--- I think the same, Tom will be fine, anyway we have to wait before going to look for him, we need more information. --- Robert argued.

--- Well OK; We're going to keep this between us without Mom finding out. --- Candileja said.

---- We will do so. --- Ana Casilda argued.

---- Let's stay in front of the television, maybe they will give new information about it. --- Robert added.

As it was proposed, they did, while the atmosphere became icy and with no intention of leaving the scene where our heroes were taken prisoner, it would be prudent to take a sidelong glance to discover that the criminals are still deep in the forest.

They went into the depth of the foil looking for a more deserted space, which would allow them to get back on the road without raising suspicions.

Then, the night had turned dark and the thick breeze, the lanterns of the car can be appretiated in the depth of the night and in the core of the forest, like the lights of a firefly.

The prisoners were still gunned down, they were studying the possibility of escaping and with this aim and they began to emit their indecipherable key where through a song they told them everything, without their executioners being able to understand anything.

That coded language that the others ignored, and that only they understood, had led them into conditioning to start an unexpected struggle between Kurt and You, while Tom clung to the neck of the Crow, the driver, causing him to lost his balance and crashed into a tree.

Manolo prevented Rey from using his weapon, while Pezuña after the impact with the tree flew out from the backfiring an uncontrolled burst that accidentally wounded Rey, in the left shoulder, while he hit the glass in front and Crow with the guide's wheel being like our heroes, taking advantage of the situation they managed to get rid of the yoke of their captors.

Despite his injury in the struggle, Rey managed to produce a shot grazing Manolo's left arm. In the midst of the confusion Tom opened the door on the left side of the passenger, managing to roll between the grasses taking the Crow's machine gun in his hands.

However, he had not realized that this machine gun lacked the comb that contained the bullets; he had rightly placed it in the vicinity of his hands.

When Manolo and You found the first opportunity, they took advantage of the confusion, also managing to escape from their captors, who had been knocked out.

The shots in the middle of the darkness alerted the patrols that had come to the fire, to realize that something was wrong, then they approached the place where the bullets were heard.

Once Rey and Kurt heard the siren, quickly taking to Cuervo and Pezuña out of space, they managed to turn on and start the vehicle, managing to escape from the place, but not before seizing the machine gun that Pezuña had been using.

When the police arrived, they had already left the contextual scene. Tom, You and Manolo appeared in front of the uniformed men and informed him about what happened.

When the situation had already been defined, the paramedics from the ambulance that had attended the scene of the fire appeared, after practicing an emergency bandage on Manolo, the paramedics collected the corpses of Cuervo and Pesuña and transferred him to the morgue.

--- We left our means of transportation in the surroundings of the scorched cabin, which has been his fate. --- You said, questioning the sergeant.

--- he is in our power; We inquired about it to find out who it belonged to and they informed us about you, We were looking for you--- The Sergeant answered with an air of a veteran.

--- Being so, mission completed, you found us --- Tom said.

--- I get the impression that it is. --- added the Sergeant with a smile on his face.

--- Thank you Sergeant, we're very grateful for his timely arrival. --- Manolo said that until that moment he had limited himself to listening.

--- Thanks, boy, how are you feeling, are you better? --- He questioned.

--- Without a doubt. --- Manolo said.

--- Well, I'm glad, I'm going to take you to the car, he is in the same place where they left him. --- the Sergeant Argued.

--- Thank you, we will appreciate it. --- You said.

--- Well, go back there. --- Added the Sergeant, opening the patrol door for him.

The special agents reciprocated the invitation; he rode in the front of the car, next to the corporal who was leading the patrol and who had already turned on the engine. They returned by the same road from which they had come followed by another patrol composed of officers without rank.

XIV

What a terrible dilemma life brings

requires me to wake up,

and when i do,

I see that it is asleep.

A month after the Sandy Hook Elementary School massacre in Newton, Connecticut, President Obama had called for a ban on assault weapons and large capacity magazines; While the National Rifle Association (NRA), had argued that Congress would not achieve either of the two things, and it was precisely when the governor of New York, Andrew Cuomo, had just signed a law nominated as the most important gun control law. strict measure of the country, whose measure had also been condemned by the NRA.

The NRA continued to press for armed guards in all schools, while the national community debated what was appropriate before such circumstance, about the type of security measure that should be taken in Public Schools in order to avoid future tragedies, however some officials like the Atlanta Public Schools Inspector that moment, proposed that schools have their own police officers.

However, according to the second constitutional amendment, the NRA insisted on defending the owners of firearms, and although some did not understand the reason for the insistence, investigations carried out in this regard revealed that the annual income of the Association by then, they were equal to $12 million contributed by the firearms industry, made up from manufacturers and sellers of firearms and ammunition; understanding that from 2005 to 2011 the NRA had received the sum of 38.9 million dollars from dozens of large companies in the arms industry, including Beretta USA; Glock, and Sturm Ruger & Co.

So in 2011, the Center for Policy Against Violence had exposed all these concerns in a study it had carried out, clearly revealing the financial ties of the NRA with the arms industry. Anyway, President Barack Obama announced a proposal for gun control, while the NRA promised the fight of the century. All this had indirectly generated a great controversy that had spread to the main sectors of society, so the California Teachers Fund, which had echoed the problem, had also chosen to withdraw its investments from the arms companies.

In addition, websites had begun to publish the lists of gun owners in New York City, expanding the effects of gun use nationwide, to the extent that there was no shortage of erudites or intellectuals who were not interested in that topic. Every day it became a real social problem.

Then the voice of Judy Willians was heard, a human rights activist who in 1977 had been awarded As a Nobel Peace Prize winner, since in previous years he had expressed concern that if the resources used for the proliferation of wars had been used to the common good or to invest it in health and education, in an attempt to reduce extreme poverty, surely the world would have entered something like the foundation of balance and hope.

She had been convinced that at that time, only the United States was spending, more than all countries combined, and argued that by 2006, the United States had spent 52 percent of its budget on defense, and only 6 percent. 3 percent on health and 5.3 percent on education, and a year later, by 2007, it had spent $ 13 million a month to sustain the Iraq war.

All this tended to cause uncertainty in those who depended on public assistance, and although what happened in Newton, were isolated events that were not generated every day; it had started to get more and more worrying and it was even believed that it could be the forecast of what would happen much more frequently in the not-too-distant future, if the societies of the world continued on that course.

The truth was, that 5 percent of the population of humanity was controlling 95 percent of all human strength, which could be giving way to the most impoverished sectors, thinking of violence as a way of the rebellion and all this would lead to justify actions aimed at generating mass murders as self-revenge, for which it was necessary to find emergency solutions that would help eradicate the scourge of violence, which firearms provided, to the detriment of the society.

Tom remembered the expression of the writer Arturo Perez Riverto, who said that "the pistol was not a firearm, but an impertinence."

He knew how much unrest firearms including explosives caused.

Recently, the death of 25 people had been reported at the headquarters of an oil company in Mexico, and later new deaths had been reported due to stray bullets and targeted shootings including one dead and two wounded in Phoenix and the fall of a teenager who had acted at the President's ascension ceremony Obama in Chicago, so it was imminent to channel the firearms control law.

In his years of service as a special agent, Tom, had faced a lot of pressure for reasons of weapons, he had been instructed in his first service by agent Rodriguez, one of the special agents, who had accompanied the President Bush Sr. on June 12, 1992, when he had gone to meet with Noriega's substitute in Panama and where, by the way, the secret service suffered great tensions with those who protested against that visit at that moment.

In addition, he had also had the experience of having accompanied President Bill Clinton on July 25, 1999, to the funeral of King Bazan of Morocco, where although nothing serious happened it was necessary to take all the precautions of place, since the worst was expected.

Agent Rodriguez's advice had been quite edifying for Tom, who in his first service on May 10, 2005, had accompanied Bush Jr. to Georgia; where a man had thrown a hand grenade, and despite not having exploded, they offered a reward of one hundred thousand dollars to whoever helped capture the person involved.

All this motivated the participation of the community, and the complaint made by a woman had led to the capture of the person involved in the failed attempt, a certain Arutunian, who before falling had murdered a local Georgia agent with a rifle. Aka 47; and the one who had been sentenced to prison for life, Tom at his age had survived more years.

After those experiences, Tom had decided to spend a little more time with the family, but that would be after Manolo left the hospital, which had been driven directly there, then he had been housed in an apartment where they would proceed to remove the bullet that it was still attached to his arm.

While Tom was on the phone with Robert from the hospital waiting room, you accompanied Manolo into the room, which Rey and Katiburo had taken advantage of to violate surveillance when he, You, was in the bathroom.

After they strangled an agent assigned to guard the area, they tried to assassinate Manolo, while Katiburo was guarding the gate, Rey had tried to assassinate him with his traditional method of suffocation, using a pillow as a tool, however as he tried, he felt the terrible pain from his wound intensify.

His left shoulder did not respond as he would like it, adding to that the unexpected appearance of You, who just in time returned from the bathroom, He had already managed to place the pillow on him, meeting resistance from Manolo who, pressing with one arm, defended himself from the purpose of Rey.

Suddenly before the shock of surprise, you shot at him, but he failed to hit him, Rey, when he was discovered, he tried to escape, then the shot caught the attention of Tom who excused himself with Robert, to find out what was happening.

---Wait, something is happening I have to leave you, we'll talk later. --- Tom said, interrupting the call.

 Although Manolo was out of danger, an exchange of gunshots broke out on the third floor, which was where he was, unbalancing the peace of the building, alarmed medical nurses and visitors ran and shouted.

The effort had hurt the wound that Rey carried on his left shoulder, but despite that he and Katiburo had decided to fight to the death, they barricaded themselves in one of the rooms of the floor, taking as hostage a patient and a nurse.

The county inspector and his agents had surrounded the Metropolitan Hospital structure; You informed the inspector through a radio in his possession about what had happened, the news broadcasts gave bulletins every five minutes according to how they received the information.

--- Surrender yourselves and we will respect your life. --- Tom said.

--- If you think you can capture us, come find us. --- Rey replied.

The nurse and the patient were crying very frightened, while You made a proposal:

--- There is no reason for innocent people to get involved, I propose an exchange, us for the hostages; It's us who they want, right? ... Then release the hostages and take us. ---You said.

--- What we want is a helicopter on the roof

A radio transmitter and a million dollars, if in twenty minutes they don't comply with our requests first we will kill the patient, then the relative and finally the nurse. --- Katiburo replied.

The inspector who was listening to the requests on the radio intervened:

--- You, open the loudspeaker so that you can hear what I'm going to say. --- the Inspector Said.

--- Very well, like this, I will ... Gentlemen pay attention that the inspector wants to tell you something. You announced.

---- we need more time to collect the million, the radio is currently being dispatched to you and the helicopter will arrive with the money in half an hour. --- The inspector promised.

---Well, they have half an hour as they require --- Rey expressed.

As time passed, the nurse bandaged the Rey's shoulder, who needed the bullet that was embedded to be extracted and for this it was necessary to attend the surgery room, which was on a different floor, and due to the circumstance that he was going through Rey, there was no way to do anything else.

During the waiting period while the inspector's men were in charge of guarding Manolo who was recovering from the surgery he had undergone for the extraction of the bullet from his arm, which at first had been thought it would be a simple scratch.

Tom placed himself on the roof of another of the buildings in a space where he could not be seen and from there he waited until Rey and Katiburo tried to board the helicopter, they were accompanied by the nurse, and the relative who had gone to visit the patient, who had been left intact in the room. When Rey and Katiburo thought they were safe, Tom shot on both of their knees causing them to lose their balance and fall on the pavement of the roof while You, who acted as a pilot with a disguise that Rey could not recognize, in fractions of seconds He threw on them disarming him while the inspector and his men arrested the criminals:

---You are under arrest, you have the right to remain silent, everything you say may be used against you, you have the right to a lawyer, if you cannot pay for one, the state will assign him to you. --- while two of his men closed the handcuffs.

The prisoners were hospitalized under a heavy contingent of guards.

President Obama in that year's State of the Union report, he alerted about the irritating culture of violence, calling for a new gun control regime, asking Congress to vote in favor of the implementation of new measures on the carrying of firearms, which included background checks and a ban on assault weapons. Faced with this prerogative, Mr. la Pierre did not find sufficient strength to oppose such provision.

Five months had passed since those events occurred, Rey and Katiburo were sentenced to twenty years, while Petroniny Gamboa had been arrested and charged with illegal arms trafficking, but his lawyer was able to demonstrate that he had all his licenses up to date for such operation, Robert and Ana Casilda got married the same day and in the same parish that Tom and Candileja got married, Manolo was Robert's best man, while You was Tom's, the weddings had been double and the party was such great that few potentates had celebrated it of that magnitude in the region.

Mrs. Bertha had attended such a great celebration, and both she and Mrs. Martha were happy; Tom and Robert alike, having the presence of their mothers, the happiest day of their existence.

Few months later the newlyweds expected new members. Strange coincidence, the sisters had married the same day and conceived the same month, which is why they had convinced Mrs. Bertha to stay with them. Tom, Manolo and You had been decorated and awarded for the order of service to the homeland, while Candileja's proposal to introduce camera in the classrooms had won in the school districts with the votes of parents and friends of the school, above of La Pierre's proposal, which insisted that armed guards be introduced into school districts.

Then everyone had come to the conclusion that information should always obey the ethics of conscience; since it was the best way to wake up one lethargic population, in the proximity of the footprint that evil leaves, on the line that divides good and bad, especially when knowledge would become the torch of peace and freedom, in a world that was dying in violence. Where many people had been trained in ignorance, to act as ignorant, those who had once been enslaved, and who had been loosed so that acting as executioners of their own people, they were eliminating the thirst for revenge that blinded them.

They had not clarified their egos for good, and, in their blindness, they served to evil; and as hatred plus hatred generated violence, they had lost the discernment of their essence and being asleep ignoring the true path, they were walking on the path of their own destruction.

Only faith in love would save them.

Arms trafficking had caused an international controversy, where the stability of nations was in danger in hands of violence.

The rulers who ruled at that time needed to stop the dangerous scourge that had crossed borders but control had already been lost, so they decided to infiltrate in the core of the messengers of evil, to limit its spread.

Gang members, obeying powerful sectors related to the mafia, contributed to the deterioration of families and the expansion of social corruption.

Tom, You and Manolo, undercover special agents, put their lives in danger in order to find a solution to the conflict and do not give up until they can send the criminals to prison.

Mariano Morillo B. prolific writer author of various genres presents us with a mixture of fiction and reality where the imagination speculates in the depth of the mind, to give an answer to social indifference.

www.ingramcontent.com/pod-product-compliance
Lightning Source LLC
Chambersburg PA
CBHW060233030426
42335CB00014B/1433